C000078316

HOW TO *PASS*

STANDARD GRADE

HOME
ECONOMICS

Alastair MacGregor

HODDER
GIBSON
AN HACHETTE UK COMPANY

Acknowledgements

The Publishers would like to thank the following for permission to reproduce copyright material:

Photo credits
Page 7 The eatwell plate, Food Standards Agency © Crown copyright material is reproduced with the permission of the Controller of HMSO and Queen's Printer for Scotland; Page 90 (top) Courtesy of Salton Europe Ltd, (bottom) © Bosch; Page 91 © Doug Cannell/istockphoto.com; Page 105 © Laila Røberg/iStockphoto.com; Page 106 (top left) Reproduced with permission, (bottom left) Reproduced with kind permission of Energy Saving Recommended scheme; Page 134 and 135 (top) Reproduced with permission of Schwartz; Page 135 (bottom) Reproduced with kind permission of Marine Stewardship Council; Page 136 (from top to bottom) (1st) Reproduced with kind permission of Soil Association, (3rd) Reproduced with kind permission of The British Toy & Hobby Association, (4th) http://ec.europa.eu/enterprise/faq/ce-mark.htm, (5th) Reproduced with kind permission of Intertek, (6th) Reproduced with kind permission of British Standards Institute; Page 137 (from top to bottom) (2nd) Reproduced with permission, (3rd) Reproduced with permission, (4th) Reproduced with kind permission of The Vegetarian Society of the United Kingdom, Ltd, (5th) Reproduced with kind permission of The Vegan Society. The Vegan Society trademark logo is a registered trademark, subject to copyright and cannot be used without the Vegan Society's permission.

All other photos © Hodder Gibson.

Acknowledgements
The questions in this book have been reproduced from Smartpapers Home Economics Question Papers with permission from Smartpapers.

The essential knowledge items on page 1 are reproduced from the Standard Grade Home Economics Arrangements document with the permission of the Scottish Qualifications Authority.

Every effort has been made to trace all copyright holders, but if any have been inadvertently overlooked the Publishers will be pleased to make the necessary arrangements at the first opportunity.

Although every effort has been made to ensure that website addresses are correct at time of going to press, Hodder Gibson cannot be held responsible for the content of any website mentioned in this book. It is sometimes possible to find a relocated web page by typing in the address of the home page for a website in the URL window of your browser.

Hachette's policy is to use papers that are natural, renewable and recyclable products and made from wood grown in sustainable forests. The logging and manufacturing processes are expected to conform to the environmental regulations of the country of origin.

Orders: please contact Bookpoint Ltd, 130 Milton Park, Abingdon, Oxon OX14 4SB. Telephone: (44) 01235 827720. Fax: (44) 01235 400454. Lines are open 9.00–5.00, Monday to Saturday, with a 24-hour message answering service. Visit our website at www.hoddereducation.co.uk. Hodder Gibson can be contacted direct on: Tel: 0141 848 1609; Fax: 0141 889 6315; email: hoddergibson@hodder.co.uk

© Alastair MacGregor 2009
First published in 2009 by
Hodder Gibson, an imprint of Hodder Education,
An Hachette UK company,
2a Christie Street
Paisley PA1 1NB

Impression number   5 4 3 2 1
Year   2012 2011 2010 2009

Cover photo Copyright 2008 photolibrary.com
Illustrations by Chris Altham
Cartoons © Moira Munro 2005, 2008
Typeset in 10.5 on 14pt Frutiger Light by Phoenix Photosetting, Chatham, Kent
Printed in Italy

A catalogue record for this title is available from the British Library

ISBN-13: 978 0340 973 882

CONTENTS

INTRODUCTION

This book gives you summary course notes for Standard Grade Home Economics, information about revision techniques and detailed advice on how to answer exam questions. It will help you to follow a study plan to achieve the best possible result in your Standard Grade Home Economics examination. In the book, the summary course content is provided in the main text, while additional advice, tips, techniques, sample questions and answers are provided in feature boxes.

Course Content

The Standard Grade Home Economics course content is split into eight areas of essential knowledge as identified below:

a. Eating a variety of foods contributes to good health

b. Current dietary advice should be considered in relation to good health

c. Individuals have varying dietary needs

d. Cleanliness is important in relation to health and well being

e. Safe practices are important in the use of resources and materials

f. Design features are an important consideration in the choice of materials and equipment

g. Individuals and families have different physical needs

h. Management of personal and household expenditure depends on priorities.

Course Elements

Whilst Standard Grade Home Economics has three Course Elements, only two are assessed in the examination: Knowledge and Understanding and Handling Information.

Knowledge and Understanding (KU)

KU accounts for approximately half of the marks in your examination paper. These questions assess your ability to recall knowledge of facts, terminology, concepts and principles, and to use knowledge of facts, terminology, concepts and principles with an explanation.

Figure 1.01

Example

Some typical KU questions might look like these:

◆ **State** one function of iron in the body.

◆ **Explain** two reasons why it is important for a family to draw up a household budget.

◆ **Identify** one safety rule to be followed when bathing a young child. **Explain** the importance of this rule.

◆ **Explain** one advantage and one disadvantage of using a credit card to purchase a mobile phone.

◆ **Identify and explain** two different lifestyle changes, other than diet, which could benefit health.

The words in green are command words. They tell you what the examiner is looking for in an answer.

Handling Information (HI)

HI accounts for approximately half of the marks in your examination paper. In these questions you will be asked to interpret and select what is relevant to a given problem or situation and then explain your choice. This might be, for example, to choose a particular product from a given range to suit a particular case study.

Figure 1.02

Example

Here are some typical HI questions:

◆ **Choose** the **most suitable** dessert for Christopher. Give four **reasons** for your choice.

◆ **Choose** one breadmaker and **evaluate** its suitability for Ryan.

◆ Yvonne wants to buy a toothbrush so that she can clean her teeth after her lunchtime break at work. **Which** toothbrush would be the **most suitable** for Yvonne?

◆ **Choose** the **most suitable** savings account for Steven.

Throughout this book you will find examples of different types of KU and HI questions, along with tips on how to answer each question.

The Examination

Your Standard Grade Home Economics examinations will normally be in April or May. It is important that you mark the date and the times of the examinations into your study guide or planner.

Remember that you will normally be sitting two examinations: Foundation and General examinations or General and Credit examinations. Make sure that you know what examination papers you are sitting.

What You Should Know

How long will each exam last?

◆ Your **Foundation** paper lasts for 1 hour. There will normally be 6 questions in this paper. The maximum number of marks will be 60, equally split between KU and HI.

◆ Your **General** paper lasts for 1 hour. There will normally be 5 questions in this paper. The maximum number of marks will be 70, equally split between KU and HI.

◆ Your **Credit** paper lasts for 1 hour and 15 minutes. There will normally be 4 questions in this paper. The maximum number of marks will be 80, equally split between KU and HI.

Revising for the examination

Your Standard Grade Home Economics examination is designed to test your knowledge and understanding across all of the eight essential knowledge (EK) statements for the course (see page 1). This book has been written with the EK in mind, each chapter being devoted to one of the eight statements. This will help with your revision, but what else should you be thinking about or doing?

1   Careful planning is important.

   ◆   Write down all the subjects that you have to revise and then rank them in order of difficulty. The ones that you find most difficult should be started earlier and also you might need to spend more time revising these subjects.

   ◆   Write down the dates of each examination.

   ◆   Now plan a revision timetable based on all the information above.

2   Your revision timetable.

   ◆   This should be based on 60–90 minutes blocks of time.

   ◆   Try to schedule revision of your difficult subjects alongside the subjects you find easier. This might make revision seem less boring and stressful.

   ◆   Remember that you can also make a timetable for your Home Economics revision. Instead of allocating time to different subjects, you can allocate time to different EK statements, spending more time on the ones that you find most difficult.

3   Revision Techniques.

Hints and Tips

There are many different ways to try to revise. Here are a few that you might find useful:

Note taking – Making brief summary notes of your course notes can be a useful method of revision. It also makes last minute revision easier as you do not have to read through pages and pages of text.

Mental maps – this is another way of taking notes. It is a diagram that is used to represent words, ideas or tasks. For more information on mental maps, visit the following website: http://en.wikipedia.org/wiki/Mind_map. An example is provided on page 20, but there are mental maps provide throughout this book.

Hints and Tips continued ➢

Hints and Tips continued

Tests – Testing yourself using questions from past papers allows you to practise exam type questions but also allows you to test how much information you can recall and use.

Summary tables or grids – these can be produced for various functions and sources, like nutrient sources, and allow for a quick overview of important facts. They can also be used to compare or evaluate information, such as features of different types of credit. See pages 9 and 47 for examples of charts and tables that have been used in this book.

Audio notes – you can make audio notes of your course notes by reading them into a Dictaphone and downloading the files onto your MP3 player. Then, you can listen to them on the bus or train!

Sticky notes – write important words of phrases onto sticky notes and put these in places that you will see every day. This helps to reinforce key words or phrases.

There are many different revision websites that provide good revision tips and advice. Type 'revision tips and techniques' into an Internet search engine to get a list of websites that offer this kind of help.

Revise now for success later!

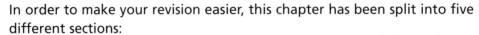

THE IMPORTANCE OF A VARIED DIET

In order to make your revision easier, this chapter has been split into five different sections:

◆ The concept of a varied diet and its relationship to health

◆ Main nutrients, their function and food sources

◆ The relationship to health of adequate intake of water and dietary fibre

◆ The relationship to health of adequate intake of energy, protein and the multi-nutrient value of food

◆ The interrelationships of groups of nutrients in relation to function.

The Concept of a Varied Diet and its Relationship to Health

Someone once said, 'We don't eat nutrients, we eat food'. To an extent this is correct, but, of course, one of the main reasons that we eat food is to get important nutrients that can be used by the body to work correctly.

There are very few perfect foods – food that will supply all the nutrients that your body requires to work correctly. However, it is the type, quantity and balance of foods that we eat that has an important role to play in ensuring we stay healthy – or not! Look at the **key words** in the box below to help you understand the concept of a varied diet.

Key Words and Definitions

Varied diet – a diet in which a range of different food is eaten. The food may not necessarily contain the correct amounts or balance of nutrients to ensure good health.

Nutrient – a substance which plants or animals need in order to grow or live.

Over nutrition – a diet that has too much of one or more of the nutrients, e.g. protein.

Under nutrition – a diet that has too much of one or more of the nutrients, e.g. fat.

Key Words and *Definitions* continued ➤

Key Words and Definitions *continued*

Balanced diet – a diet in which a range of food is eaten to ensure it provides an adequate amount of nutrients and energy to meet the body's needs and ensure good health.

Malnutrition – a diet that has a lack of sufficient nutrients or an imbalance of nutrients to maintain a healthy body.

It can be difficult to try to make the correct choices when selecting food to eat in order to achieve a good and varied diet. The Eat Well Plate is a pictorial attempt by one government agency, the Food Standards Agency, to show how people can achieve a balanced diet.

The Eat Well Plate tries to encourage people to choose a variety of foods from different food groupings. We are encouraged to eat more of those foods in the largest sections of the plate:

◆ bread, rice, potatoes and pasta (and any other starchy foods)

◆ fruits and vegetables.

We are encouraged to eat moderate amounts of the sections of the plate which include:

◆ milk and dairy foods

◆ meat, fish, eggs and beans (and other non-dairy sources of protein).

We are encouraged to eat food from the section of the plate which shows foods containing fat and foods and drinks containing sugar, the least.

Figure 1.01
The Eat Well Plate

HOW TO PASS STANDARD GRADE HOME ECONOMICS

Questions and Answers

F The following is a handling information (HI) type question that might appear in a Foundation paper:

Study the Eat Well Plate on the previous page.
List two foods that would appear in one of the following food groups:

◆ meat, fish, eggs, beans (and other non dairy sources of protein)

◆ fruits and vegetables.

As this is a HI question, the answers are provided in the chart or illustration provided. You need to study the chart carefully and then extract the correct information from it.

Sample Answer:

In this case, the answers might include salmon, eggs, red kidney beans, sardines and beef (steak) for the first group, and grapefruit, broccoli, banana, carrots, spring onions and tomatoes for the second group.

Remember that these are foods which must appear in the diagram provided. You will get no marks for writing down foods which do not appear in the diagram.

Key Words and Definitions

Fat Soluble: vitamins stored in the fat content of foods

Water Soluble: vitamins stored in the water content of foods

Main Nutrients, Their Function and Food Sources

There will always be questions in the examination paper about the function of nutrients and the main food sources of these nutrients. In the Credit paper, the range of nutrients that you have to study is greater.

The nutrients listed in Table 1.1 can be tested in any examination. Those with the Credit mark, **C**, however, will only ever be tested in the Credit paper.

Table 1.1

Nutrient	Function(s) in body	Main food source
Protein	◆ Growth, repair and maintenance of body tissues ◆ Secondary source of energy	Eggs, meat, fish, milk, cheese, soya and soya products
Carbohydrate	◆ Main source of energy for the body ◆ Excess energy is stored as fat and so provides warmth	Pasta, cereals, bread, vegetables, fruit, sugar and products containing sugar, flour and products containing flour
Fat	◆ Main source of energy for the body ◆ Warmth ◆ Provides fat soluble vitamins (A,D, E and K)	Oil, butter, margarine, meat, full-cream milk, cheese, cream, peanuts

Vitamins can be fat soluble or water soluble.

Fat soluble vitamins

Vitamin A	◆ Assists with bone and tooth development ◆ Promotes good night vision ◆ Maintains healthy skin and membranes ◆ Helps to resist infection	Offal (e.g. liver), egg yolk, dark green vegetables (e.g. broccoli), orange coloured fruits and vegetables (e.g. apricots, peaches, tomatoes), full-cream milk
Vitamin D	◆ Assists with bone and tooth development ◆ Required for effective blood clotting ◆ Assists in absorption of calcium	Milk, margarine, offal (e.g. liver), salmon, tuna, egg yolk. Note: sunlight produces vitamin D in the skin
Vitamin E	◆ Has a role to play in red blood cell development ◆ Works in partnership with Vitamin K ◆ Assists in the maintenance of cell membranes	Vegetable oil, nuts, green leafy vegetables, fortified cereals, margarine
Vitamin K	◆ Assists in the clotting of blood ◆ Linked to the development of strong bones	Green leafy vegetables, vegetable oil, cereals, dairy foods

Water soluble vitamins

Vitamin B	◆ Release of energy from food ◆ Maintain healthy nerves ◆ Required for cell reproduction	Meat, fish, nuts, wholegrains, green leafy vegetables, liver

Table 1.1 *continued*

C	Vitamin B1	◆ Release of energy from carbohydrates ◆ Promotes growth and appetite ◆ Maintains a healthy nervous system	Offal (e.g. liver), pork, wholegrain bread and grain products, cereals, nuts, green vegetables
	Vitamin B2	◆ Release of energy from carbohydrates, protein and fat ◆ Maintains healthy skin and eyes	Offal (e.g. liver), white flour, wholegrain flour, bread, milk, egg whites
	Folic Acid (Vitamin B9) (Folate)	◆ Needed in the formation of red blood cells and body cells ◆ Reduces the risk of neural tube defects in pregnancy	Liver, kidney, kiwi fruit, dark leafy vegetables, peanuts, wholegrain cereal and products
	Vitamin C	◆ Helps to absorb iron from food sources ◆ Helps prevent infections ◆ Helps with the repair of cuts and wounds	Fruits (e.g. kiwi fruit, blackberries and apples), citrus fruits (e.g. oranges) and vegetables such as broccoli, peas, potatoes, spinach, carrots

Minerals

	Iron	◆ Required for the formation of red blood cells	Liver, meat, beans, nuts, dried fruits, wholegrains (e.g. brown rice), fortified breakfast cereals
	Calcium	◆ Helps build strong bones and teeth ◆ Helps the blood to clot ◆ Helps with muscle control	Milk, cheese, dairy food, green leafy vegetables
	Fluoride	◆ Helps to develop strong teeth ◆ Helps prevent tooth decay	Fish, tea, drinking water
	Sodium (salt)	◆ Helps to keep the fluid balance in the body correct ◆ Helps with muscle function ◆ Helps with nerve function	Processed foods, salt, bacon, crisps and snack products like peanuts
C	Phosphorus	◆ Helps build strong bones and teeth ◆ Helps to release energy from foods	Red meat, dairy foods, fish, poultry, bread, rice and oats

The Interrelationship of Nutrients

Whilst the body needs many different nutrients to function correctly, it also relies on different nutrients working together. In your Credit examination paper, you might be asked specific questions about the interrelationship of nutrients – i.e. how certain nutrients need to work together in order to function properly. It is therefore important not just to know about the function of each individual nutrient, but also which ones work together.

Calcium, phosphorus and vitamin D

Vitamin D is required to maintain the correct balance of calcium and phosphorus in the body. Both calcium and phosphorus are important in the formation of strong bones and teeth and this healthy formation is dependent on the correct amounts of both nutrients being available. Vitamin D helps to regulate their absorption.

Iron and vitamin C

Vitamin C helps the body absorb iron, particularly iron from plant sources. Vitamin C assists in the conversion of iron into a form that can be easily used by the body.

Remember, if you are being asked a question about the interrelationship between nutrients, it is important that you do not just restate the individual functions of each nutrient. You must explain how they work together in the body.

Key Words and Definitions

Free radicals: the natural by-products of the body turning food into energy. Free radicals are highly dangerous and are linked with diseases such as cancer, heart disease and premature ageing.

Table 1.2

Term	Description	Sources
Antioxidants (also known as vitamins)	Chemical compounds which can bind themselves to free radicals so preventing damage to cells. Antioxidants help to deactivate free radicals. Vitamins A, C and E are often referred to as antioxidants. Different antioxidants work in different ways and so the key is to eat as wide a range as possible.	Foods rich in vitamins A, C and E. Other antioxidants, which are not vitamins, include lutein, lycopene and selenium.

Key Words and Definitions continued ➤

THE IMPORTANCE OF A VARIED DIET

Key Words and Definitions continued

Table 1.3: Carbohydrates (saccharides)

Term	Description	Sources
Monosaccharides	A simple sugar. Mono means one and saccharide means sugar. There are three monosaccharides.	See below
Disaccharides	This is a type of carbohydrate which is made up of two monosaccharides. Di means two and saccharide means sugar.	Table sugar is the most common disaccharide.
Polysaccharides	This is a type of complex carbohydrate. Poly means many and saccharide means sugar. Starch is the main type of polysaccharide. There are other more complex types of carbohydrates which the body cannot digest – these are commonly known as non starch polysaccharides (NSP), or dietary fibre.	Starch. Fruits and vegetables and wholegrain cereal products are rich in NSP.

Table 1.4: Fatty acids

Term	Description	Sources
Fatty acid	Fat is an essential nutrient to the body. The problem with fat is that when we eat too much or eat the wrong types they negatively affect our body. Fatty acids are the simplest unit of fat.	Any food containing fat.
Saturated fatty acids	These are generally regarded as having a possible negative effect on health. Saturated fats are usually solid at room temperature.	Generally found in foods of animal origin e.g. meat and dairy produce.
Mono unsaturated fatty acids	This type of fat is regarded as being 'healthier' than saturated fats. Unsaturated fats are normally liquid at room temperature.	Found in foods such as olives, rapeseed and linseed.
Polyunsaturated fatty acids	This type of fat is regarded as a 'healthier' type of fat. Unsaturated fats are normally liquid at room temperature.	Certain types of margarine, sunflower seed oil.
Essential fatty acids	The body can make most of the fatty acids that it needs. Those that it cannot manufacture itself are known as essential fatty acids and therefore must be obtained through food intake.	Mainly from oily fish.

Questions and Answers

G Nutrition is a popular topic in exam papers. A typical question is shown below:

State one function of vitamin C in the body. (General KU 1 mark)

This is a typical question which relies on you recalling ('state') your knowledge of nutrients. You would not generally be asked to provide more than two functions for a particular nutrient. As this question is only worth 1 mark, you only need to provide one function.

C However, some Credit level questions may ask you to use your knowledge to provide a more detailed answer:

Identify two antioxidant vitamins and give two explanations why a diet high in antioxidants contributes to good health. (Credit KU 4 marks)

This question asks you to recall your knowledge ('identify') and then use your knowledge ('explanations') to link the benefits of antioxidants to health. The question is worth 4 marks; 1 mark is awarded for each correctly identified antioxidant and 1 mark awarded for each correct explanation.

Sample Answers:

In this Credit question, vitamin A, vitamin C or vitamin E would each be awarded 1 mark to a maximum 2 marks.

- *A diet rich in antioxidants can help in the prevention of certain types of cancers.*
- *A diet rich in antioxidants can help prevent heart disease.*
- *A diet rich in antioxidants can help prevent premature ageing of the skin.*
- *A diet rich in antioxidants can help reduce the action of free radicals and so prevent heart disease/cancer/premature ageing.*

Each explanation would attract 1 mark to a maximum of 2 marks.

The Relationship to Health of Adequate Intake of Water and Non Starch Polysaccharide (NSP)

We know that nutrients are important if the body is to function correctly. Water and NSP are not nutrients, but they are two important requirements if the body is to function well.

Water is essential for human life. It is required in the formation of body fluids such as blood, sweat and mucous membranes. Additionally, it regulates body temperature through perspiration. The main source of water is through drinking water, but it is also obtained through foods like fruits, meat and milk.

Non Starch Polysaccharide (NSP), also known as dietary fibre, cannot be digested from food and so is not classified as a nutrient. It is very important to the body, though, as it absorbs water, making faeces softer and easier to remove from the body. It helps prevent constipation, diverticular disease and certain types of bowel disease, like bowel cancer. A diet rich in NSP is linked with lower cholesterol levels. NSP is the indigestible, fibrous part of fruits, vegetables and cereals, so the best sources are foods like oats, pears, broccoli and beans.

The Relationship of Adequate Intake of Energy, Protein and the Multi-Nutrient Value of Food to Health

Energy

Energy is not a nutrient; it is a by-product of the breakdown of food by the body. This energy is then used by the body to carry out all of its functions and activities. Excess energy is stored as fat in the body and so it is very important that you obtain an energy balance: that is, where the amount of energy that is provided by the food we eat equals the amount of energy that we burn through daily activity and exercise. The energy balance can be affected by:

◆ insufficient energy intake in relation to body activity and exercise. This could leave you feeling tired and listless and could, in the longer term, lead to being underweight and other health problems.

Figure 1.02

◆ excess energy intake in relation to body activity and exercise. This could mean that your body stores the excess energy as fat. In the longer term this could lead to you being overweight or even obese.

Figure 1.03

Protein

We have seen that excess energy is stored as fat in the body. Likewise, any excess protein that cannot be used for growth, repair or maintenance of body tissue is converted to energy. If this energy cannot be used by the body, it will be stored as fat and again could lead to being overweight or obese in the longer term.

Multi-nutrient value of foods

Most foods contain a variety of different nutrients. If we eat a wide variety of foods, we can normally obtain all the nutrients that the body needs in order to function properly. Sugar is one of the few foods that contains just one nutrient – carbohydrate – and so is of limited value to the body. This is one of the reasons why it is recommended that we keep our intake of sugar low.

Questions and *Answers*

Here are some sample nutrition-based questions that illustrate the types of questions that you can expect in an exam.

Bread is a good source of carbohydrate.
Give two uses of carbohydrate in the body. (Foundation/General KU 2 marks)

This is a two mark Foundation/General level KU question which is testing your ability to recall information. The initial statement about bread is not core to the question; it is there to lead on from a previously asked question about bread. This question is simply asking you to provide two functions of carbohydrate in the body. You would be given 1 mark for each use (function).

Sample answers:

♦ *Major source of energy.*

♦ *Excess can be converted to fat and used for warmth.*

Another question might be:

Explain the following terms:
Under nutrition
Over nutrition (General level KU 2 marks)

This is a two mark General level KU question, again asking you to recall knowledge.

Questions and *Answers* continued ➤

THE IMPORTANCE OF A VARIED DIET

Questions and **Answers** continued

G

Sample answers:

Under nutrition

◆ *lack of nutrients in the diet*

◆ *lack of one or more nutrient in the diet*

◆ *poor health resulting from the depletion of nutrients due to inadequate nutrient intake over time*

Over nutrition

◆ *excess nutrients in the diet*

◆ *an excess of one or more nutrient in the diet*

◆ *a condition associated with diseases such as obesity*

◆ *long-term consumption of excess nutrients*

1 mark is awarded for each point of explanation for each term.

Summary

What you need to know!

◆ Nutritional terminology

◆ The major nutrients – sources and functions

◆ The interrelationship of nutrients – Credit only

◆ Water and NSP – sources and functions

Chapter 2

CURRENT DIETARY ADVICE IN RELATION TO GOOD HEALTH

We are told that healthy eating is not hard to do and that the benefits are well worth the effort involved, but why should we be following a healthy diet, and what does this really mean for the types and amounts of food that we eat?

Healthy eating can help:

◆ control weight

◆ your general health

◆ reduce the risk of developing illness and serious diseases.

In order to achieve a healthy diet, there are some basic rules that need to be followed in order to meet Scotland's current dietary targets. These are explained below. Everyone needs to know the text in black. The text in red should be known by those undertaking General level. The text in green should be known by those undertaking Credit level.

As a nation, Scotland should be working to:

◆ *reduce* our intake of fat. **Intake of total fat should reduce to be no more than 35% of energy intake**

◆ *reduce* our intake of sugar. **Adult intake should not rise. Child intake should reduce to no more than 10% of energy**

◆ *reduce* our intake of salt. **Average intake should reduce from 163 mmol to 100 mmol per day**

◆ *reduce* our intake of alcohol

◆ *increase* our intake of fruit and vegetables. **Intake to double to 400g per day**

◆ *increase* our intake of bread. **Intake to increase by 45% from present daily intake**

◆ *increase* our intake of breakfast cereals. **Double to 34g per day**

◆ *increase* our intake of total complex carbohydrates (fruits and vegetables, bread, breakfast cereals, rice, pasta and potatoes). **Increase by 25%**

◆ *increase* our intake of fish, especially oily fish. **Intake of white fish to be maintained. Intake of oily fish to double to 88g per week.**

Key Points

These terms have a similar meaning:

◆ Healthy eating
◆ Current dietary targets
◆ Scottish dietary targets

Questions and Answers

F This is a three mark, Foundation level, KU question related to your knowledge of the Scottish dietary targets.

Mark is a student and he buys the following foods when he goes shopping:

◆ Canned tuna fish   ◆ Wholemeal bread
◆ Low fat spread   ◆ Apples

Choose **three** of the foods from above and for **each** state which Scottish dietary target it helps to meet.

You have the opportunity to select three of the four foods provided. Select the foods that you are most confident about answering correctly. You then need to state which dietary target each food relates to. These questions are designed to test your knowledge of the Scottish dietary targets and so you should not be providing the same answer for each food you select!

As this is a Foundation level question, you would not be expected to provide a lot of detail in your answer.

Questions and **Answers** continued ➢

Questions and Answers continued

F **Sample answers:**

Canned tuna fish

◆ Eat more fish

◆ Eat more oily fish

Wholemeal bread

◆ Eat more bread

◆ Increase intake of bread – mainly using wholemeal and brown bread

◆ Eat more Total Complex Carbohydrates

Low fat spread

◆ Eat less fat

◆ Eat less fat, especially saturated fat

Apples

◆ Eat more fruit

◆ Eat more fruit and vegetables

1 mark for correct target which must be accurately quantified i.e. use of words such as 'more', 'less'. Total of three marks available.

But how easy is it to follow these guidelines? The mental map in Figure 2.1 shows ways in which you can achieve these healthy eating targets. In an examination, you would not normally be expected to provide more than four specific examples of how to achieve a specific dietary target.

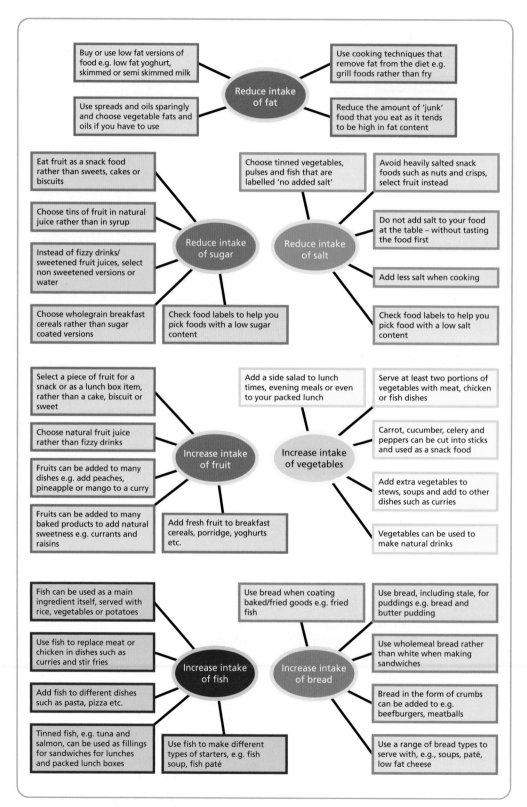

Figure 2.1 Mental map

A note about alcohol

Alcohol is energy rich and can be associated with health problems. In cookery, most alcohol is burned off during the cooking process. Use non or low alcohol alternatives in cookery, or substitute with fruit juice or stock if a recipe suggests alcohol.

Of course, the type of cooking method that you use to cook food will also have health implications. Look at table 2.1 for information on how cooking methods affect the nutritional value of the food we eat. But what else affects nutrient loss?

Heat

◆ Heat destroys vitamin B.

◆ Vitamin C is sensitive to low temperatures.

Alkalinity

◆ Alkalines destroy vitamin B1.

◆ Alkalines increase the loss of vitamin C.

Solubility

◆ Vitamins B and C dissolve in water.

◆ Cooking in water for a long time destroys vitamins B and C.

◆ Cooking in a large amount of liquid will mean greater loss of vitamins B and C.

◆ Vitamins A and D dissolve in fat.

◆ Fat loss means vitamin A and D loss.

Table 2.1

Methods	Description	Fat content	Nutrients
Grilling	Cooking food under direct heat of a grill. Fat drips from the food into the grill tray. You may have to lightly brush some foods with oil prior to grilling to prevent the food from drying out	Normally reduced	Some heat-sensitive nutrients lost
Frying	Cooking food in fat or oil. Can be shallow frying (small amount of oil used) or deep frying (food immersed in oil)	Increased	Some heat-sensitive nutrients lost
Baking	Cooking food in an oven	Stays the same as no fat added during the cooking process	Some heat-sensitive nutrients lost
Steaming	Cooking food in steam	Stays the same as no fat added during the cooking process	No loss

Table 2.1 *continued*

Methods	Description	Fat content	Nutrients
Stir frying	Only a little amount of oil is needed. This is a very quick method of cooking	Increased by a small amount	Minimal loss
Poaching	Gentle method of cooking food in a liquid	Stays the same as no fat added during the cooking process	No loss
Boiling	Cooking in boiling water. If the cooking liquid is used for gravy, then nutrient loss can be minimised	Stays the same as no fat added during the cooking process	Some loss of water soluble nutrients
Stewing	Cooking food gently in water which is just below boiling point. If the cooking liquid is used for items like gravy, then nutrient loss can be minimised	Stays the same as no fat added during the cooking process	Some loss of water soluble nutrients
Microwave cooking	Cooking food in a microwave oven. This is a quick method of cooking	Some loss of water soluble nutrients	Minimal loss

Remember

Whilst a healthy method of cooking may be selected, it is the foods that are incorporated within the recipe that will determine overall healthiness. Baking a sugar rich meringue is a healthy method of cooking, but the food being baked is high in sugar!

Questions *and* Answers

The following question is a Credit level KU question, worth three marks. The question relates to dietary advice. You need to have a good knowledge of the Scottish dietary targets in order to answer this question. This is not simply a recall question; you are expected to use your knowledge of the targets. When answering this question, you should think about the context – school lunches.

The following statements are taken from a report which gives advice on how to ensure that school lunches meet current dietary targets.

State **one** reason for each point of advice.

Questions and *Answers continued* ➢

Questions *and* Answers *continued*

c **Statement 1**

Where confectionery is being sold it should be placed away from the food service points.

Statement 2

Oil-rich fish should be served once a week.

Statement 3

Rice and pasta should each be offered a minimum of once a week.

Sample answers:

Statement 1

◆ *It means that children will not be attracted to sugary/sweet/fatty foods as they will be less noticeable/less easily available.*

◆ *Children will not be encouraged to impulse buy sweets just because they see them next to the service point.*

◆ *This will discourage purchase as part of a meal and so help to achieve the Scottish dietary target to reduce sugar intake/reduce fat intake.*

Statement 2

◆ *This will encourage the purchase of oily fish products as part of a school meal so assisting with the Scottish dietary target to increase oily fish consumption.*

◆ *Oily fish contains protective fatty acids that are missing from the Scottish diet and so their consumption should be encouraged.*

◆ *Many children are unfamiliar with this type of fish product and so this may encourage them to sample/taste such foods.*

◆ *Provides variety in the diet of schoolchildren.*

Statement 3

◆ *To provide an alternative/variety to fried potatoes; provides variety in the diet of schoolchildren.*

◆ *This will encourage the purchase of products rich in total complex carbohydrates as part of a school meal so assisting with the Scottish dietary target to increase total complex carbohydrate consumption.*

◆ *Some children are unfamiliar with this type of product and so this may encourage them to sample/taste such foods.*

1 mark for each reason linked to each statement. Total of 3 marks.

The Relationship Between Diet and Health

Eating a well balanced diet and following current dietary advice can assist in the prevention of many diseases and health problems. Below are common ailments that are directly related to diet.

Anaemia

Anaemia is caused by a lack of iron in the diet. Symptoms of the condition include tiredness, breathlessness and dizziness. Iron is used to make a substance in the blood that carries oxygen around the body. A lack of iron means that the body cannot move as much oxygen as it needs.

Anaemia can also be caused by a lack of vitamin B12 or folic acid in the diet. Vitamin B12 anaemia causes possible damage to nerves, a sore tongue, pigmented skin, possible night blindness and can cause depression. Folic acid anaemia can cause foetal abnormalities, including spina bifida.

Bowel disorders

Bowel disorders are commonly caused by a diet which is lacking in NSP/dietary fibre, although there can be other causes. Table 2.2 lists typical conditions and symptoms related to bowel disorders.

Table 2.2

Condition	Symptoms
Constipation	The inability to pass waste products (faeces) out of the body. Associated with a diet low in NSP. Faeces tend to be hard and dry and difficult to pass from the body. NSP helps with the absorption of water so making faeces softer and easy to pass through the digestive system.
Piles	These are enlarged and misshaped blood vessels surrounding the anus (bottom). Associated with a diet low in NSP. If constipated, the extra effort (pushing) required to remove faeces from the body causes pressure on the blood vessels surrounding the anus, resulting in piles.
Cancer	Bleeding from the anus, diarrhoea or constipation are the most common symptoms, but it is important to remember bowel cancer is more common in people over the age of 60. NSP helps to ensure that waste products pass through the bowel quickly, so minimising the long term risk of cancer.
Diverticular disease	Disease of the large intestine. Small pouches develop which can cause abdominal pain, cramps, bloating and excess wind. Associated with a diet low in NSP and often associated with long term constipation.

Table 2.2 *continued*

Coronary Heart Disease (CHD)	This is a condition whereby fatty deposits stick to the blood vessels (arteries) supplying the heart. This reduces the blood and oxygen supply to the heart and reduces its ability to function properly. Main symptom is angina (severe pain in the chest, spreading to the arms) caused by lack of oxygen reaching the heart muscle.
Hypertension	Also known as high blood pressure. Whilst our blood pressure changes on a daily basis, hypertension is when blood pressure remains constantly high mainly as a result of thickening and hardening of the artery walls. This increases the risk of coronary heart disease.
Stroke	This is a loss of brain function due to a disruption of the supply of blood (and therefore oxygen) to the brain. A stroke is very serious and can lead to death. Strokes can be associated with high blood pressure, but are also associated with other medical conditions.
Tooth decay	Also known as dental caries. Tooth decay is caused by the action of acid producing bacteria which feed on any tiny deposits of food remaining on your teeth after eating. The bacteria produce acid which dissolves the lining (enamel) of the tooth. Often caused by a lack of dental hygiene – inadequate or non brushing of teeth is the main cause. It is best to avoid sugary foods and drinks and remember to brush your teeth at least twice a day using fluoride toothpaste.
Obesity	Obesity is a heavy accumulation of fat in the body, to an extent that it leads to poor heath. Obesity may be linked to a medical condition or it may simply be due to a case of overeating and lack of exercise. Obesity is associated with other health conditions such as stroke, CHD, diabetes and certain types of cancer.

Key Words

★ **CHD:** Coronary Heart Disease   ★ **NSP:** Non Starch Polysaccharide

Key Words and Definitions

Atherosclerosis: hardening of the arteries which be may the result of high blood pressure and which can result in coronary heart disease or stroke.

Whilst diet is a major factor in each of the diseases identified above, there are other contributing factors to ill health:

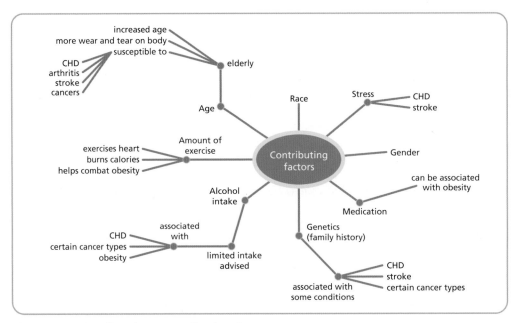

Figure 2.2 Diet disorders: contributing factors

Questions and Answers

G This is a KU question from a General paper worth 4 marks: 2 marks for the factors and 2 marks for the linked reasons. In this question, you are using recall of knowledge about factors affecting choice, as well as using your knowledge to provide an explanation.

Ray sometimes cooks for his friends.

List **two** factors that Ray should consider when **choosing** foods for his friends.

Explain why **each** factor should be considered.

Sample answers :

Age – Different age groups may have different food tastes e.g. older may have more traditional preferences.

Gender – Males and females require different portion sizes and so Ray would need to ensure that sufficient food has been bought to feed the composition of friends he has invited.

Questions and Answers continued ➤

Questions *and* Answers *continued*

G *Health – If any of the friends have special dietary requirements through health problems/issues, then these would need to be considered to ensure food was suitable.*

Available income – Ray should be certain he buys food that fits in with his available budget/financial circumstances.

Available equipment – Ray should be able to cook/store/prepare the foods selected.

Available skills – This ensures that the foods that are selected are able to be cooked/stored/prepared by Ray.

Likes and dislikes of guests should be considered:

◆ *so that his friends will eat the food that has been prepared*

◆ *to ensure that food is not wasted through not eating*

◆ *so that his friends will realise that he has gone to some effort to make suitable foods.*

Nutrition – Ray may wish to be sure that the foods selected for the meal are nutritionally balanced/provide a balanced meal/contain a variety of nutrients for his friends.

Healthy eating – Ray may wish to be certain that the foods selected for the meal meet with some of the Scottish dietary targets to ensure his friends' good health.

In some questions, you may be asked to link together different areas of course content in one question. In this next example, not only have you to recall information about Scottish dietary targets, you also have to relate these to health implications. Here is a KU question from a General paper worth 6 marks.

A café is trying to meet Scottish dietary targets and is offering the following meal:

Steamed Salmon
served with
Roasted Mediterranean
vegetables and
deep fried potatoes

Figure 2.3 Restaurant menu

Choose **two** foods from the meal which help to meet a **different** Scottish dietary target.

Explain why **each** choice improves health.

In this question you will get marks for

◆ correctly identifying foods which contribute to Scottish dietary targets (total 2 marks)

Questions and Answers continued ➢

Questions and Answers continued

G
- identifying the linked Scottish dietary target (total 2 marks)
- providing an explanation as to why this choice of food might improve health (total 2 marks).

Remember to try to show your knowledge by not repeating the same dietary target.

Sample answers would include:

Salmon

Dietary target: Intake of oily fish to double/intake of oily fish to double to 88g per week.

- *Rich in protein which is used for growth/repair/maintenance of tissue/secondary source of energy.*
- *Source of omega 3 fatty acids which can help reduce cholesterol/help prevent heart disease/prevent inflammation diseases.*
- *Source of vitamin D which helps the body absorb calcium.*

Vegetables

Dietary target: Intake of (fruit and) vegetables to double/intake of (fruit and) vegetables to double to 400g per day.

- *Contain NSP which can help prevent a range of bowel disorders, constipation, bowel cancer, diverticular disease, piles, varicose veins.*
- *Contain NSP which fills you up so avoids snacking which can lead to obesity.*
- *Low in sugar so preventing tooth decay/obesity.*
- *Low in fat so preventing obesity/heart disease.*
- *Low in salt so preventing hypertension/strokes/heart attacks.*
- *High in vitamin C which is required to help absorb iron/prevent scurvy/prevent infection.*

Questions and *Answers* continued ➤

Questions and Answers continued

G | *Potatoes*

Dietary target: Intake of total complex carbohydrates to increase/intake of total complex carbohydrates to increase by 25%.

- *Contain NSP which can help prevent a range of bowel disorders, constipation, bowel cancer, diverticular disease, piles, varicose veins.*
- *Contain NSP which fills you up so avoids snacking which can lead to obesity.*
- *Low in sugar so preventing tooth decay/obesity.*
- *Low in salt so preventing hypertension/strokes/heart attacks.*
- *High in vitamin C which is required to help absorb iron/prevent scurvy/prevent infection.*
- *Good source of carbohydrate for energy/warmth.*

Note: the potatoes are deep fried so are 'unhealthy'. However, potatoes are a total complex carbohydrate (TCC) and so using the TCC target is appropriate.

Summary

What you need to know!

- Dietary targets
- Ways to meet dietary targets
- Cooking methods
- Relationship between diet and health

- Dietary diseases
  - Anaemia
  - Bowel diseases
  - Cancers
  - Coronary heart disease
  - Stroke
  - Tooth decay
  - Obesity

THE VARYING DIETARY NEEDS OF INDIVIDUALS

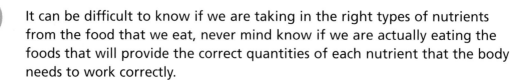

It can be difficult to know if we are taking in the right types of nutrients from the food that we eat, never mind know if we are actually eating the foods that will provide the correct quantities of each nutrient that the body needs to work correctly.

Key Words

★ **DRV:** Dietary Reference Value

★ **EAR:** Estimated Average Requirement

★ **RNI:** Reference Nutrient Intake

★ **LRNI:** Lower Reference Nutrient Intake

Dietary Reference Values

Dietary Reference Value (DRV) is the collective term used to indicate the amounts of energy and nutrients required by different groups of healthy people in the UK:

Estimated Average Requirement (EAR) – the estimated average need for a nutrient, especially energy. Some people may need more, some people may need less.

Reference Nutrient Intake (RNI) – the estimated amount of a nutrient that would meet the needs of most people in the UK.

Lower Reference Nutrient Intake (LRNI) – the estimated amount of nutrients that would meet the needs of only a very few people in the UK.

In examinations you may be asked specific questions relating to the individual needs of different groups of people.

Infants

Infants are classified as children under the age of one, or at the earliest stage of life. There are no differences in the nutritional requirements between infant girls and boys except for energy:

Figure 3.1 Infant

EAR of energy for boys under 1	545–920 kcal per day
EAR of energy for girls under 1	515–865 kcal per day

The reason for this difference is that, on average, boys tend to be some 300g heavier than girls and so require an additional energy source.

The diet of an infant in the first few months of life is milk, either breast milk from the mother or formulae milk from a bottle. 'Breast is considered best' because:

◆ Breast milk is individualised for the baby, providing the correct composition and proportion of nutrients for the baby's needs.

◆ Breast milk is free.

◆ Breast milk needs no preparation and is provided at the correct temperature and consistency, without the hassle of having to sterilise bottles and accessories.

◆ Breast milk contains important antibodies that protect the baby's immune system.

◆ Breast feeding helps to create a strong bond between mother and child.

Children

By children, we mean boys and girls between the ages of 1 and 10. Within this age range there is a significant amount of body growth and development requiring an increase in all the major nutrients. There are also some differences between the sexes in this age range.

Figure 3.2 Young child

Age	EAR	RNIs									
Sex	Energy Kcal/ day	Protein g/day	Vit A µg/day	Vit B1 Mg/day	Vit B2 Mg/day	Niacin Mg/day	Vit C Mg/day	Vit D µg/day	Calcium Mg/day	Iron Mg/day	Sodium Mg/day
Boys 1–3	1230	14.5	400	0.5	0.6	8	30	7.0	350	6.9	500
Girls 1–3	1165	14.5	400	0.5	0.6	8	30	7.0	350	6.9	500
Boys 4–6	1715	19.7	500	0.7	0.8	11	30	–	450	6.1	700
Girls 4–6	1545	19.7	500	0.7	0.8	11	30	–	450	6.1	700
Boys 7–10	1970	28.3	500	0.7	1.0	12	30	–	550	8.7	1200
Girls 7–10	1740	28.3	500	0.7	1.0	12	30	–	550	8.7	1200

Table 3.1 DRVs for young people

The main differences in the nutritional needs of individuals in this age range are as follows:

Protein – Required for the growth of body tissues, as this is a time of major growth and development. The protein needs increase with age.

Energy – Not only do we need more energy as we age, but because they tend to be more active than females, boys require greater energy intake than girls.

Calcium – As the body grows and develops, the need for strong bones and teeth means that we need to increase our intake of calcium.

Iron – as our body grows, we require more blood which is able to carry oxygen around the body. For this reason our intake of iron needs to increase.

Other nutrients – given that this is a period of body growth and development, our bodies need an increased supply of all nutrients, with the exception of vitamin C and D.

Adolescents

By adolescent, we mean the age range between 11 and 18. This is the second main phase of body growth and development and so our nutritional needs increase.

Figure 3.3 Adolescent

Age	EAR	RNIs									
Sex	Energy Kcal/ day	Protein g/day	Vit A µg/day	Vit B1 Mg/day	Vit B2 Mg/day	Niacin Mg/day	Vit C Mg/day	Vit D µg/day	Calcium Mg/day	Iron Mg/day	Sodium Mg/day
Boys 11–14	2200	42.1	600	0.9	1.2	15	35	–	1000	11.3	1600
Girls 11–14	1845	41.2	600	0.7	1.1	12	35	–	800	14.8	1600
Boys 15–18	2755	55.2	700	1.1	1.3	18	40	–	1000	11.3	1600
Girls 15–18	2110	45.4	600	0.8	1.1	14	40	––	800	14.8	1600

Table 3.2 DRVs for adolescents

Protein – Required for the growth of body tissues, as this is a time of growth and development. The protein need increases with age for both sexes. Males require more protein than females due to the fact that males have an increased body mass and generally larger body frames than females.

Energy – Not only do we need more energy as we age, but because they tend to be more active than females, boys require a greater energy intake than girls.

Iron – Not only do adolescents need more iron with age, but girls also have a greater requirement than boys. This is due to the loss of monthly menstrual blood in adolescent girls.

Other nutrients – all other nutrients (with the exception of sodium and vitamin D) are required in greater quantities with age. With the exception of iron and vitamin C, boys have a greater nutrient requirement than girls.

Adults

When we reach adult life, our body has peaked in relation to growth and development and nutrients are required for maintenance and repair.

Figure 3.4 Adult

Age	EAR	RNIs									
Sex	Energy Kcal/ day	Protein g/day	Vit A µg/day	Vit B1 Mg/day	Vit B2 Mg/day	Niacin Mg/day	Vit C Mg/day	Vit D µg/day	Calcium Mg/day	Iron Mg/day	Sodium Mg/day
Men 19–50	2550	55.5	700	1.0	1.3	17	40	–	700	8.7	1600
Woman 19–50	1940	45	600	0.8	1.1	13	40	65+	700	14.8	1600
Men 50+	2550	53.3	700	0.9	1.3	16	40	–	700	8.7	1600
Woman 50+	1900	46.5	600	0.8	1.1	12	40	65+	700	8.7	1600

Table 3.3 DRVs for adults

Protein – Protein need in adults reduces with age as they require less for growth but still have a requirement for repair and maintenance of body tissues.

Energy – in comparison to adolescents, the energy requirements of adults are lower for both men and women, although men require more energy than women because they are generally regarded as being more active and having bigger body frames to carry about.

Calcium – In comparison to adolescents, there is a reduced need for calcium, again because growth and development will have ceased.

Iron – There is a reduced requirement for men after age 19 as growth rate will have peaked. The iron content for women remains unchanged from teenage years and is higher than males due to iron loss in females as a result of menstruation.

Example

Below is a typical HI question from a Credit level paper. There will normally be one of these questions in a Credit paper. To answer this question you need to know not just about nutrients, but also about the dietary needs of individuals. This is an easy type of question to pick up marks, but only if you have revised well.

C A school group is going to a ski competition and consists of six boys aged between 11 and 14 years. The group stop at a café and have lunch.

Taking account of the Dietary Reference Values (DRVs) for this age group and the contribution that lunch should make to the daily nutritional requirement for this age group, evaluate the suitability of this lunch.

Example continued ➤

Example *continued*

C

Dietary Reference Values for Males aged 11–14 years in the UK per day					
Estimated Average Requirements	Reference Nutrient Intakes				
Energy	Protein (g)	Calcium (mg)	Phosphorus (mg)	Vitamin C (mg)	Vitamin B1 (mg)
2200 kcal	42.10	1000	775	35.00	0.9

Table 3.4

The lunch should provide approximately 1/3 of day's requirements i.e.:					
Energy	Protein (g)	Calcium (mg)	Phosphorus (mg)	Vitamin C (mg)	Vitamin B1 (mg)
740 kcal	14.03	333	258	11.67	0.3

Table 3.5

Dietary analysis of the lunch					
Energy	Protein (g)	Calcium (mg)	Phosphorus (mg)	Vitamin C (mg)	Vitamin B1 (mg)
720 kcal	19. 5	612	156	12.00	0.1

Table 3.6

If you can master this type of question, you can be guaranteed full marks when you encounter one like it in the exam. Although it is a HI question, it specifically asks you to **evaluate** the suitability of the lunch for the specific group or person in the case study. This means that you have to state not only why the meal would be a good choice for the group, but also why it might not be a good choice. You also need to ensure that in your answer you refer back to the information provided in the case study.

So where do you start with this type of question?

1 Start by reading the case study or situation that you have been given.

2 Highlight or underline the important bits of information in the case study. This has been done in the case study above with bold text.

3 Use the information presented to answer each part of the question. This question is worth 12 marks:

Example *continued* ➤

Example *continued*

c

4 marks for explaining how the meal does/does not meet DRV.

4 marks for explanations relating to the function of the nutrient.

4 marks for the consequences to the skier of having not enough/too much of the nutrient.

The sample answers here provide an example of the types that will be acceptable:

Energy

DRV: The lunch does not have enough energy in relation to the DRV.
Function: Energy is required for physical activity/all body activity.

Consequences

◆ Skiers are active and a lack of energy could lead to tiredness/loss of weight/irritability/weight loss for this age group and will adversely affect their performance.

◆ Skiers will be using additional energy and a lack of energy from the lunch may well adversely affect performance in the skiing competition.

Protein

DRV: The lunch provides more than the required DRV for this age group.
Function: Protein is required for growth, repair and maintenance of body cells.

Consequences

◆ The lunch provides more than the required DRV for this age group. This is not a problem as members of this age group are still growing and so their development will not be hampered.

◆ Protein is used for growth and repair of body tissues, and if a member of this age group becomes injured during skiing, they will have enough protein to ensure adequate repair.

◆ Protein is used as a secondary source of energy and for this age group of skiers this will work to their advantage, as they are currently low in energy intake.

◆ Protein is used as a secondary source of energy and for this age group of skiers this will work to their advantage. As they are currently low in energy intake, this may help with their performance in the ski competition.

Calcium

DVR: The lunch provides more than is required to meet 1/3 of DRV.
Function: Calcium is required to develop strong bones and teeth.

Example *continued* ➤

Example *continued*

c **Consequences**

- The lunch provides more than is required to meet 1/3 of DRV. This will not be a problem as calcium is required to maintain strong bones and skiers will need strong bones to ski/will help to reduce possibility of breakage/injury/will help with strengthening bones to prevent injury.

- The lunch provides more than is required to meet 1/3 of DRV. This will not be a problem as any excess will be secreted so causing no long term side affects for this age group.

- The lunch provides more than is required to meet 1/3 of DRV. This will not be a problem as members of this group are still developing and growing and calcium is important for the development of strong bones/strong teeth.

- Calcium is required for the clotting of blood and if the skiers fall/get injured and suffer a cut, then blood clotting should not be problematic as there is plenty of calcium in this lunch.

- Calcium is required for the normal functioning of muscles and skiers will be using their muscles constantly/need strong muscles, and this lunch provides enough calcium to ensure that this is not a problem.

- Calcium is required for the normal functioning of nerves and this is important to skiers who need to react quickly to events and as the diet contains enough calcium this is not a problem.

Note: you would continue with this same pattern of answers for the other nutrients in the lunch: phosphorus, vitamin C and vitamin B1.

In this type of question it is also an idea to indicate that this evaluation is only a snapshot of the nutritional intake of the skier and that, when all meals for the day or week are taken into account, the evaluation may change.

Key Words *and* Definitions

Osteoporosis: A medical condition where the bones become thin, weak and break easily.

Osteomalacia: A medical condition where bones become weak. This is the adult form of rickets where the bones soften during development.

The elderly

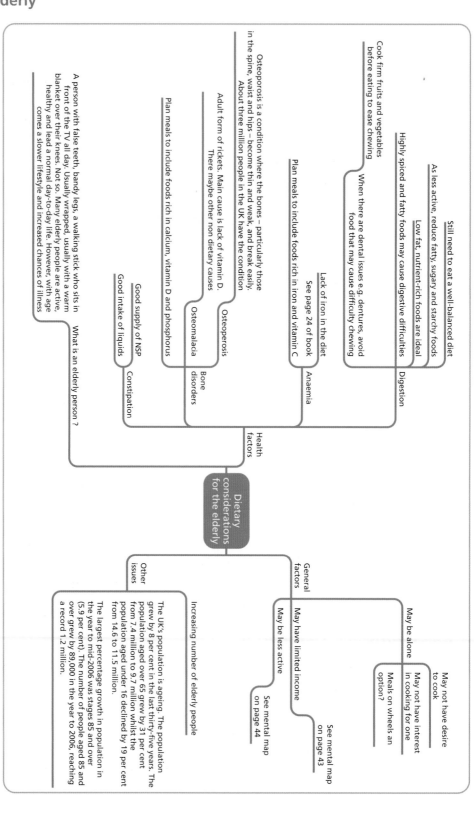

Figure 3.5 Dietary considerations for the elderly

Other groups who may have specific dietary requirements

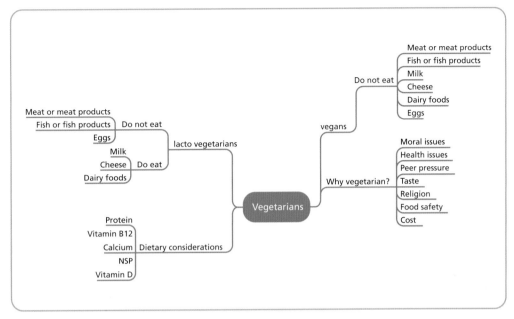

Figure 3.6 Vegetarians

Vegetarians

There are two main types of vegetarians: lacto vegetarians and vegans.

Figure 3.6 shows many of the different reasons why people become vegetarian.

Why vegetarian?

◆ Moral issues – some people believe that intensive food production has a negative effect on the welfare of animals.

◆ Health reasons – some people believe that following a vegetarian diet is healthier due to the rich sources of fruit and vegetables in the diets and the reduction of animal fat and dairy foods.

◆ Peer pressure – it may be that a person becomes a vegetarian because they think it is fashionable or because their friends are vegetarian.

◆ Taste – some people do not like the taste or texture of meat.

◆ Religion – some religions have rules that ban the eating of animal products because it means that an animal has to die to produce the food item. Many Hindus and Buddhists are vegan.

◆ Food safety – some people believe that chemicals, growth hormones, use of pesticides and the recent Foot and Mouth disease scare all mean that foods which derive from animals may have a health risk.

◆ Cost – some people say that it is uneconomic to produce plants to feed to animals when the plants could be eaten instead.

HOW TO PASS STANDARD GRADE HOME ECONOMICS

Dietary considerations for vegetarians

◆ **Protein** – Animal products are an excellent source of protein. If these are excluded from the diet, then a varied supply of vegetable based protein foods is required to ensure that protein DRVs are achieved.

◆ **Vitamin B12** – This vitamin is not found in plant foods. Anyone following a vegetarian diet, particularly a vegan diet, should ensure that they consume foods that are fortified with vitamin B12 (has this vitamin added already) or consume vitamin B12 supplements.

◆ **Calcium** – Dairy foods are an excellent source of calcium. If these are excluded from the diet, then calcium should be obtained from eating a variety of fruits, vegetables, pulses and nuts. It is important to remember that some of these sources may contain a substance called phytic acid which prevents the body from absorbing calcium.

Key Words and Definitions

Phytic acid: a substance found in plants which prevents the absorption of calcium.

◆ **NSP** – A vegetarian diet can be rich in NSP due to the amount of fruits and vegetables being consumed. This can have added health benefits such as regular bowels movements and the reduction of cholesterol in the body.

◆ **Vitamin D** – Vitamin D is found in dairy foods but in very few plant foods, therefore the main source of vitamin D for vegetarians will be sunlight.

Example

F This is a typical Foundation level KU question which is testing your ability to recall basic information about vegans.

(a) List **two** foods that should be avoided by a vegan. (KU 2 marks)

(b) Give **one** reason why a person might become a vegan. (KU 1 mark)

Part (a) is asking you to provide a list of two foods that a vegan would not eat. You would gain 1 mark each for providing any two the following answers:

◆ meat/meat products

◆ milk/milk products/dairy foods

◆ cheese/foods containing cheese

◆ eggs/foods containing eggs

Example continued ➤

Example continued

F

◆ fish/foods containing fish

◆ gelatin/foods containing gelatin

Part (b) is asking you to give one reason why a person might become a vegan. Again, this is a recall question. You would gain 1 mark for providing any one of the following answers:

◆ believe that it is wrong/not moral to kill animals for food

◆ believe that it is uneconomical to use animals for food

◆ dislike of the taste of animal products

◆ religion may dictate not eating animal foods

◆ peer pressure may force people to turn vegan to fit in

◆ health reasons may dictate a vegan diet

◆ belief that vegan diet may be a safer diet due to issues such as BSE/Foot and Mouth disease

Pregnant women

It is important that women who are planning to become, or who are already, pregnant try to follow a healthy diet.

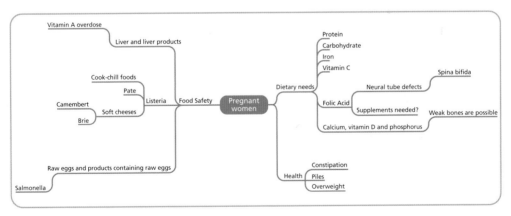

Figure 3.7 Pregnant women

Key Words *and* Definitions

Haemorrhoids/piles: swollen blood vessels in the anal canal and lower rectum causing pain, itching and possible bleeding.

Dietary needs of women who are pregnant

◆ **Protein** – the protein needs are increased as a result of the growth of the developing foetus (baby).

◆ **Carbohydrate** – the energy needs are increased as the mother will need to supply energy to the developing foetus. However, the mother's activity level will also decline, so the saying 'you should be eating for two' is, in fact, not true.

◆ **Iron** – As a result of the menstrual cycle (periods) stopping during pregnancy, there is no increased requirement for iron. However, the mother's blood supply is used to supply the developing foetus with nutrients including iron. The baby will require a supply of iron to last the first few weeks after birth and for this reason iron intake should remain constant

◆ **Vitamin C** – Eating foods which are rich in vitamin C will assist with the absorption of iron. Vitamin C is also required for the development of the tissues of the foetus.

◆ **Folic Acid** – is essential for the health of the growing baby. A diet rich in folic acids is known to prevent neural tube defects, such as spina bifida, in the developing baby. Folic acid supplements may be advised by medical practitioners.

◆ **Calcium, vitamin D and phosphorus** – are essential not just for the maintenance of a strong skeleton and teeth for the pregnant woman, but also to ensure the development of a skeleton in the foetus. Any lack of calcium for the developing baby will mean that calcium will be extracted from the pregnant woman's bones, possibly causing weakness in bone structure.

◆ **NSP** – Constipation and piles are common in pregnancy. A lack of NSP can cause constipation and the associated stress caused by constipation can lead to the development of piles (haemorrhoids), which can be uncomfortable.

Other concerns for pregnant women

◆ **Weight** – it is important that a pregnant woman maintains an appropriate body weight. Excess weight can cause additional health problems with a pregnancy, as can being underweight. The old tale that you 'need to eat for two' is not accurate. You need to eat a healthy balanced diet to meet the needs of yourself and the developing baby.

◆ **Liver and liver products** such as liver paté have a high vitamin A content which can be harmful to the developing baby.

◆ **Soft cheeses** such as Brie and Camembert may contain bacteria called *Listeria* which can harm the developing baby. Other products such as cooked meats, chilled sandwiches and paté may also be a source of *Listeria*.

◆ **Raw eggs** and products containing raw eggs should be avoided as they may contain dangerous bacteria such as *Salmonella*, which can cause damage to the developing baby.

There are many factors which affect food choice for everybody.

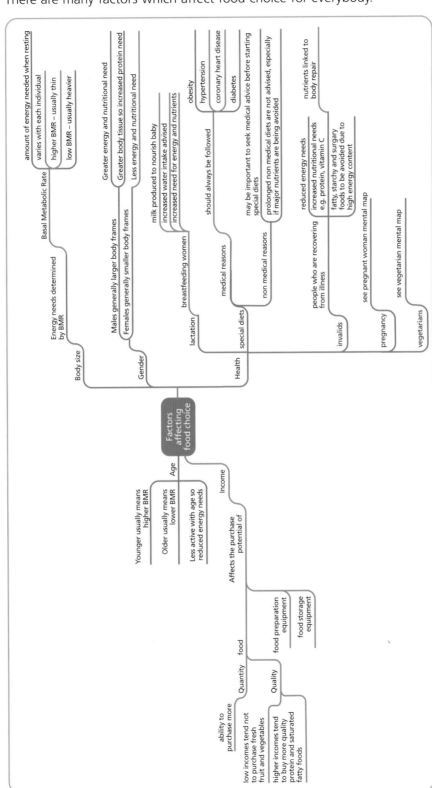

Figure 3.8 The importance of food choice

Our lifestyle also plays a part in our food choice.

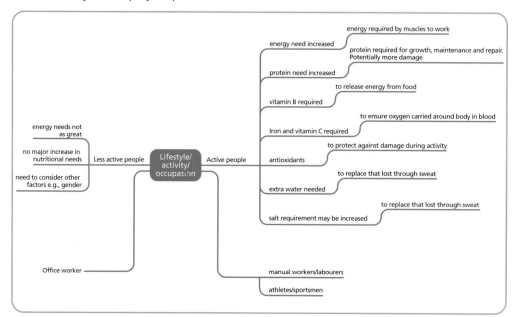

Figure 3.9 The importance of lifestyle choice

Summary

What you need to know!

Dietary requirements of individuals:

◆ Infants

◆ Children

◆ Adolescents

◆ Adults

◆ Elderly

◆ Vegetarians

◆ Pregnant women

Factors affecting food choice.

Chapter 4

THE IMPORTANCE OF CLEANLINESS IN RELATION TO HEALTH

In order to make your revision easier, this chapter has been split into eight different sections:

◆ General personal hygiene

◆ Clothing care

◆ Hygiene in relation to food handling

◆ Causes, effects and control of food spoilage

◆ Food storage and preservation

◆ Food poisoning

◆ Cross-contamination of food

◆ Refrigeration and freezers.

General Personal Hygiene

There is a saying that 'cleanliness is second only to godliness'. This means that having a clean body and taking care of your appearance is very important. Here are the main rules for good personal hygiene:

Figure 4.1

1 Wash your body regularly, ideally every day. This removes any dirt, grease and any stale sweat.

2 Wash hands after visiting the toilet and before eating a meal. This removes any bacteria transferred to hands after visiting the toilet.

3 Wash hair regularly to remove dirt, grease and sweat.

4 Comb or brush your hair regularly to ensure good health.

5 Brush teeth daily, ideally twice a day, to prevent bad breath and tooth decay.

6 Visit the dentist on a regular basis, ideally twice a year. Remember that dental check-ups are free on the NHS.

7 Visit the optician every two years for an eyesight test. Remember that eyesight tests are free on the NHS.

So why are these steps so important?

Our bodies are naturally covered in bacteria. These bacteria feed on the sweat generated from our bodies. If not removed through regular washing, the bacteria produce smelly gasses. This results in body odour, sometimes known as BO.

Clothing Care

It is as important to take care of your clothing as it is to take care of your body. Clothing provides protection to your body from natural elements. Clothing can also be expensive to buy, so this is another good reason to take care of it.

Clothing should be:

◆ washed or cleaned regularly

◆ dried carefully

◆ ironed if required

◆ stored in an appropriate manner.

To help you look after your clothes, a standard international labelling scheme has been introduced to help the consumer take care of the clothing that they buy. This is known as care labelling. The following charts detail each of the labels in the scheme and give information about the specific instructions that each label provides.

Instructions designed to help you wash clothing

The labels are based on a set of symbols which represent a washing tub.

Symbol	What the symbol tells us	Suitable types of clothing	Comments
	This item can be washed at a temperature of 60°C.	Sheets, pillowcases towels and some types of underwear.	Can be washed at full machine cycle.
	This item can be washed at a temperature of 60°C.	Sheets, pillowcases towels and some types of underwear.	The solid bar under the wash tub indicates that the item must be washed on a reduced or gentle cycle.
	This item can be washed at a temperature of 50°C.	Items made from polyester and cotton/polyester mixtures.	The solid bar under the wash tub indicates that the item must be washed on a reduced or gentle cycle.
	This item can be washed at a temperature of 40°C.	Items made from cotton.	Can be washed at full machine cycle.
	This item can be washed at a temperature of 40°C.	Items made from acrylic, acetate, nylon, triacetate, cotton/acrylic mixtures, polyester/ viscose mixtures.	The solid bar under the wash tub indicates that the item must be washed on a reduced or gentle cycle.
	This item can be washed at a temperature of 40°C.	Items made from wool and wool mixtures.	The broken bar under the wash tub indicates that the item must be washed on a very gentle or delicate cycle.
	This item can be washed at a temperature of 30°C.	Many clothing items labelled with a higher temperature can be washed at 30°C.	The solid bar under the wash tub indicates that the item must be washed on a reduced or gentle cycle.
	Hand wash only.	Delicate items.	
	Do not wash.		

Table 4.1

Instructions designed to help you dry clothing

When wet, some fibres can be easily damaged. For this reason certain items will require to be dried in a particular way. These labels are based on a set of symbols which represent a drier.

Symbol	What the symbol tells us
	Item can be tumble dried.
	Item can not be tumbled dried.
	Item should be drip dried.
	Item should be line dried after removing excess water.
	Item should be dried flat after removing excess water.

Table 4.2

Instructions designed to help you iron clothing

After washing and drying, clothing may crease. Ironing helps to smooth out the fibres in the item. It is important to iron an item at the correct temperature in order to:

◆ successfully remove creases

◆ prevent damage to the item, such as burning or melting.

These labels are based on a set of symbols which represent an iron.

Symbol	What the symbol tells us	Suitable items
	The item can be ironed using a hot iron (210°C).	Suitable for items made from cotton, linen and viscose.
	The item can be ironed using a warm iron (160°C).	Suitable for items made from polyester mixes.
	The item can be ironed using a cool iron (120°C).	Suitable for items made from acrylic, nylon acetate and triacetate.
	The item should not be ironed.	

Table 4.3

Instructions designed to help you bleach clothing

White clothing can easily stain, and marks from grass or food might be hard to get out. Bleach can be used to removed these stains. It needs, however, to be used carefully to prevent damage to the items.

These labels are based on a set of symbols represented by a triangle.

Symbol	What the symbol tells us
	The item can be bleached.
	The item should not be bleached.

Table 4.4

Instructions designed to help you dry clean clothing

Not all items can be cleaned in the traditional way. In such cases, and normally for items which are delicate or which have special finishes, dry cleaning may be an option. Dry cleaning is usually undertaken by specialist cleaners. These labels are based on a set of symbols represented by a circle.

Note: you do not need to know the chemical names of the dry cleaning solvents for the exam.

Symbol	What the symbol tells us
	The item can be dry cleaned.
	The item can be dry cleaned in any solvent.
	The item can be dry cleaned in fluorocarbon and petroleum solvents only.
	The item should not be dry cleaned.

Table 4.5

THE IMPORTANCE OF CLEANLINESS IN RELATION TO HEALTH

Questions *and* Answers

G If you were to be asked about laundry symbols in an exam, it is likely that you would be asked to identify and explain the meaning of a symbol. Alternatively, the symbols may appear in a HI question. It is therefore important to know what each symbol means. A typical question is shown below. This is a three mark KU question from a General paper, and tests your ability to recall information. You would get 1 mark for a correct explanation of each symbol.

Explain the information provided by each symbol.

Symbol 1   Symbol 2   Symbol 3

Sample answers:

Symbol 1: Clothing/textile items/fabric can be tumble dried.

Symbol 2: The clothing/textile item/fabric should not be/must not be/can not be washed.

Symbol 3: Clothing/textile items/fabric can be dry cleaned. Or, clothing/textile items/fabric can be dry cleaned using all cleaning solvents.

Remember

Keep in mind that, although there are 24 different symbols to know, if you remember the function of each shape, this makes the task a lot easier.

Washing   Dry Clean   Iron   Bleach   Drying

Hygiene in Relation to Food Storage

Bacteria are all around us. Not only on our skin and clothes, but on all surfaces. Some bacteria are harmful; most are safe. Food hygiene and safety is all about trying to prevent harmful bacteria from causing illness.

Food hygiene rules can be categorised as:

Personal hygiene rules – those rules that apply to the person preparing or cooking food.

Kitchen hygiene rules – those rules that apply to the environment in which you are preparing or cooking the food.

Table 4.6: The list of rules below have been classified as either P (for personal hygiene) or K (for kitchen hygiene)

Classification	Hygiene rule

P	Wash hands regularly to reduce the spread of bacteria:
	◆ Before
	  ○ preparing food
	  ○ eating
	◆ Between handling foods, especially raw foods
	◆ After
	  ○ handling raw foods, especially meat, fish and poultry
	  ○ visiting the toilet
	  ○ coughing or sneezing
	  ○ touching your hair

P	Nails should be clean and kept short to prevent: ◆ dirt being stored behind long nails ◆ nails breaking and falling into food Nails should not be painted with nail varnish as this may flake off into food and contaminate it.
P	Hair should be washed on a regular basis and long hair should be tied back to prevent it falling into food. A hair net or other form of headwear should be worn to prevent hair dropping into food.
P	Protective clothing should be worn in order to: ◆ prevent transfer of bacteria from outer clothing to food ◆ protect clothing from spills.
P	Wounds should be covered with a waterproof coloured plaster. This allows the plaster to be easily located should if fall off.
P	Jewellery should be removed to ensure that: ◆ gems/stones do not fall out into food ◆ bacteria which may be trapped in the jewellery does not contaminate food.

P	Do not prepare or cook food if unwell, especially if you have a stomach or bowel disorder. All illness should be reported to a supervisor.
K	Pets should not be allowed in the kitchen and should not be used as the place to feed pets as they can carry bacteria and disease.
K	Wipe up all spills as they happen, not only to prevent the possible spread of bacteria, but spills can attract flies and insects and can be a safety hazard.
K	Dispose of all rubbish and waste carefully in order to prevent the spread of bacteria and also to reduce the possibility of attracting flies and insects. Ensure that all rubbish bins are emptied on a regular basis and have well fitting lids.
K	Kitchens should be designed to have separate washing facilities for food and for hands. This helps prevent contamination from one to the other.
K	Food should be kept covered at all times in order to prevent contamination from flies, insects etc.
K	All work surfaces should be cleaned on a regular basis. The motto 'clean as you go' should be followed.
K and P	Smoking is not permitted in the kitchen. Not only is there a risk of cigarette ash contaminating food, the act of smoking may transfer bacteria from mouth to hand and then hand to food.
K	Disposable cloths should be used for drying hands to minimise the spread of bacteria.
K	Any infestation of pests, e.g. flies, insects, birds, should be reported to the environmental health department as this can pose a health risk.
K	The kitchen should be designed to ensure: ◆ good lighting to prevent eye strain and also to ensure good cleaning ◆ good ventilation to ensure comfortable work conditions and minimise warm, damp conditions in the kitchen which might promote bacterial growth.

Questions and Answers

F   Below is a Foundation level KU question worth 4 marks. This question is asking you to use your knowledge of personal and kitchen hygiene. It relates to making sandwiches for a packed lunch, so you should keep this in mind when answering the question. You would get 1 mark for each rule. Make sure that in your answer you provide two kitchen hygiene rules and two personal hygiene rules.

Questions and *Answers* continued ➢

Questions and Answers continued

F List **two** personal hygiene and **two** kitchen hygiene rules that should be followed when making sandwiches for a packed lunch.

Sample answers:

Personal hygiene rules:

- *Remove all jewellery before preparing sandwiches.*
- *Cover cuts/boils/skin infections before preparing sandwiches.*
- *Wash hands/nails before/during/after preparing sandwiches.*
- *Wash hands after visiting the WC if preparing sandwiches.*
- *Remove nail varnish.*
- *Tie hair back or use a hair net/chef's hat.*
- *Wear clean protective clothing.*
- *Do not cough/sneeze over sandwiches.*
- *Use disposable paper tissues to dry hands.*
- *Do not use fingers to taste fillings for the sandwiches.*

Kitchen hygiene rules:

- *Dispose of all waste immediately.*
- *Waste bins should have well fitting lids.*
- *Separate facilities for washing food and hands.*
- *Separate cloths for hand drying and equipment drying.*
- *Cover foods at all times.*
- *Adopt a 'clean as you go' approach to hygiene.*
- *Wipe all spills immediately.*
- *Do not smoke in the kitchen when preparing sandwiches.*
- *All work surfaces should be cleaned before/after use.*
- *All equipment should be cleaned after use.*
- *Animals/pets must be excluded from the kitchen.*
- *Use only products that are within their use by/best before date.*

Causes, Effects and Control of Food Spoilage

> ### Key Words and Definitions
>
> **Food spoilage:** the process leading to a food deteriorating in quality so that it cannot be eaten.
>
> **Food contamination:** the presence of any unacceptable or harmful substance in a food item.
>
> **Food poisoning:** an illness caused by eating food which has been contaminated with pathogenic bacteria.
>
> **Pathogen:** a micro-organism which can cause illness or disease.

What are the characteristics or effects of food spoilage?

◆ The food has an unusual smell, often due to the action of bacteria on the food.

◆ The food has an unusual texture, such as being slimy due to bacterial contamination.

◆ The food has a change in colour. Such a result might be from mould growth.

◆ The food has a change in flavour; for example, milk which has gone sour.

What causes food spoilage?

There are three main types of micro-organism that contribute to food spoilage: bacteria, moulds and yeast.

Bacteria

Bacteria are single celled organisms that are so small they cannot be seen by the naked eye. Some bacteria are useful to us in that they can be used for:

◆ the manufacture of food items such as cheese, yoghurt and beer

◆ the manufacture of medicines

◆ assisting with digestion.

However, while some bacteria are useful to the body, some can cause illness and disease. These are know as pathogenic bacteria. Illnesses like food poisoning are caused by toxin producing bacteria.

Moulds

Moulds are another form of micro-organism which can cause food spoilage. Moulds are a type of fungus. Many moulds are visible to the naked eye, especially when they have had the opportunity to grow and develop.

Like bacteria, some moulds can be used in beneficial ways:

◆ Some moulds are used in cheese production to produce a strong flavour and colour.

◆ Penicillin was developed from mould.

Yeasts

Yeasts are single-celled organisms that can cause food spoilage. Yeast usually affects foods such as jam and meat, and usually affects the flavour.

Like bacteria and moulds, yeast can be used in food and drink manufacture. Two very common uses are in the manufacture of:

◆ wine

◆ bread.

Conditions required for bacterial growth

There are certain conditions that allow micro-organisms to grow and multiply. In these conditions bacterial growth is rapid and can lead to food spoilage quickly. The ideal conditions for micro-organism growth include the availability of nutrients, moisture and warmth. If you remove any one of these conditions for growth, bacterial multiplication can be significantly reduced.

Availability of food

Bacteria prefer foods which are rich in protein, such as chicken, fish, milk, cheese and eggs. But other foods, like cooked rice, gravy and pies, can be a great environment for growth. These are known as high risk foods.

Key Words and Definitions

High Risk Food: a food which is an ideal ground for breeding bacteria.

Danger zone: temperature between 5°C and 63°C, which is an ideal temperature for bacteria to multiply.

Dormant: bacteria which are not active or growing but can be active or growing at a later time.

Temperature

Bacteria need warm conditions in order to multiply and grow. Ideal temperatures for bacterial growth are between 5°C and 63°C, this is known as the **danger zone**.

Below this temperature, bacterial growth begins to slow down. At freezing point, bacteria become dormant – they cannot grow or multiply, but remain alive. Above the danger zone, bacteria begin to die.

Time

Bacteria need time to grow and multiply. In ideal conditions, one bacterium can multiply very quickly. Within 15 minutes, some bacteria can multiply into two separate organisms. This means that if we started with 2 bacteria, in 4 hours there might be 131,072!

Other factors

Moisture – We know that humans need water to survive. Likewise, bacteria need a source of water to live, grow and reproduce.

pH – The pH of a substance tells you whether it is an acid or alkaline. Bacteria prefer an acidic pH of between 4.5 and 7.

Air – Most bacteria need air (oxygen) to exist. These are known as aerobic bacteria. However, some bacteria can survive and multiply without the presence of oxygen. These are known as anaerobic bacteria.

Key Words *and* Definitions

Aerobic bacteria: bacteria which require oxygen to multiply.

Anaerobic bacteria: bacteria which do not require oxygen to multiply.

Spore: special type of bacterial cell that allows bacteria to survive in unsuitable conditions.

What You Should Know

Spores – Some bacteria are able to produce spores when conditions for multiplication are not suitable. A spore is a special form of bacteria that can survive unsuitable conditions and is capable of growing into a bacterium when conditions become suitable.

Enzymes – This is a type of protein that is used to make chemical changes in plants and animals. Some enzymes can make food spoil. Enzymes in fruits make the fruits ripen. Some enzymes, like those found in pineapple, can be used to tenderise meat.

Example

G This is a KU question from a General paper and is worth 2 marks. The question asks you to recall knowledge relating to factors affecting bacterial growth. You are provided with two factors and you have to explain the effects of each on bacterial growth.

Explain the effect of each of the following factors on the growth of bacteria:

(i)   Warmth

(ii) Moisture.

Answer:

Warmth

◆ *Encourages/promotes the growth of bacteria.*

◆ *Within the danger zone, 5°C–63°C, bacterial growth is increased/promoted.*

◆ *Excessive warmth – above 63°C – will kill some bacteria.*

Moisture

◆ *Moisture promotes/encourages/increases bacterial growth.*

◆ *A lack of moisture will discourage/decrease/reduce bacterial growth.*

◆ *No moisture will prevent bacterial growth.*

Questions and Answers

G Food hygiene and safety can also be the context for HI questions. The following question is a 5 mark question from a General paper and is split into three parts. In part 1 you have to select the most suitable product for the given situation. For part 2 you have to provide reasons for your choice. For part 3 you have to select a product for a different situation.

! Remember that in these questions you should underline or highlight the important points in the case study, as you should refer to them in your answer. In this example, these points are highlighted in bold.

Questions and Answers continued ➢

Questions and Answers *continued*

G Ray likes to keep his house clean.

He is looking to buy a **value for money** cleaning product that he can use in his house.

Ray wants to use a product that will **not scratch** and which can be used on **plastic, metal and wooden surfaces.**

Ray does **not like to use products which contain bleach** or are **harmful to the environment**.

Study the information about cleaning products below.

Information about cleaning products			
	A	B	C
Suitable for use on	All household surfaces except stainless steel	Wood Plastic	All household surfaces
Environment friendly	✱✱	✱	✱✱✱
Cost	8 pence per use	4 pence per use	5 pence per use
Additional features	◆ pack of 50 disposable wipes ◆ a non–bleach product ◆ wipes made from a non-scratch material ◆ wipes come in a refillable pack ◆ kills 99% of all bacteria	◆ cream cleaner in a squeeze bottle ◆ contains 10% bleach ◆ not suitable for some surfaces as product may scratch ◆ cleaner comes in a plastic container ◆ non-drip cap	◆ cleaning solution in a spray gun container ◆ a non–bleach product ◆ a liquid based product which will not scratch ◆ refills can be bought ◆ orange scented
Safety information	◆ non-irritant	◆ may irritate skin	◆ keep out of reach of children
Key: ✱ poor ✱✱✱ excellent			

(a)   State which cleaning product would be the **most suitable** for Ray?

(b)   Give three reasons for your choice.

When answering this question, you need to match up the best choice of product to meet the specific needs of Ray – i.e. the parts you have highlighted.

Questions and **Answers** *continued*

(c) Mary is a single parent with a three year old son. Mary wants a cleaning product that will remove germs from the toilet seat in the bathroom.

State which cleaning product would be the most suitable for Mary?

This is a different situation but uses the same table. Again, you should underline the main points that you need to consider. These questions are designed to ensure that you select a different response from the previous choice. You should not be selecting the same product twice.

Sample answers:

*(a) Correct choice – Cleaning product **C** – 1 mark for the correct choice*

(b) Reasons for choice

◆ *The cleaning product can be used on all household surfaces, which makes it a good choice for Ray as he wants to use it specifically on plastic, metal and wooden surfaces.*

◆ *The cleaning product has an excellent environment friendly rating, which makes it a good choice for Ray as he is looking for a product which will not harm the environment/which does not damage the environment.*

◆ *The cleaning product has a relatively low cost and this is good for Ray as he is looking for a product that is value for money.*

◆ *The cleaning product costs 1p per use more than the cheapest product but is more environmentally friendly and Ray may be prepared to pay this extra cost as he wants to care for the environment.*

◆ *The cleaning product is contained in a spray gun container and this type of product may be more environmentally friendly than other products like aerosols and so is suitable for Ray who wants to protect the environment.*

◆ *The cleaning product is a non-bleach product and so suits Ray's needs as he does not want a product containing bleach.*

◆ *The cleaning product does not scratch surfaces and this means that the product will be suitable for Ray and the wooden, plastic and metal surfaces that he wants to clean.*

◆ *Refills can be bought for this cleaning product meaning that the original container will not be disposed of, which makes it environmentally friendly.*

Questions and **Answers** *continued* ➢

THE IMPORTANCE OF CLEANLINESS IN RELATION TO HEALTH

HOW TO PASS STANDARD GRADE HOME ECONOMICS

Questions and *Answers continued*

Remember that you only need three reasons from the comprehensive list of reasons above. It is always good practice to relate your answers back to the information provided in the case study.

The minimum acceptable answer for this type of question would be: *The cleaning product has an excellent environment friendly rating*. However, it is good practice to relate your answer back to the information in the case study, as in the examples above.

For part (c) of the question, the correct choice is cleaning product **A**. You would gain 1 mark for this choice.

You do not have to provide justification for your answer. However, the main reason why you would select product A is that it is the only product that says it kills 99% of bacteria (she wants to remove all germs) and can be used on all household surfaces (she wants to use in on the toilet seat).

Food Storage and Preservation

Key Words and *Definitions*

Blanching: immersing food in boiling water for a short time before cooling rapidly in cold water.

Food preservation is the process of extending the life of foods by controlling the factors that cause food spoilage, such as temperature, time and bacteria. In Table 4.8, different methods of preserving food are described.

Method	Factor which is controlled	Description	Suitable foods
Freezing	Temperature Moisture	Reduces storage temperatures to below −18°C. Bacteria become dormant. Water is converted to ice so water becomes unavailable. Blanching fruits and vegetables before freezing destroys enzymes.	Most foods except those with a high water content e.g. tomatoes

Once food has defrosted, bacteria can begin to multiply. For this reason you should never refreeze food that has been defrosted. The lower the freezer temperature, the smaller the ice crystals in the food, the less damage there is to the food. Strawberries, for example, when frozen and then defrosted may have a mushy texture because the ice crystals have damaged the cell walls of the fruit. Freezing at low temperatures minimises tissue damage.

Method	Factor which is controlled	Description	Suitable foods
Chilling	Temperature	Reducing storage temperatures to below 5°C. Bacterial multiplication slows down. Bacteria are not dormant and so the food will eventually spoil.	Dairy foods, salad produce, meat, fish
Jam making	pH Temperature	Initial boiling of fruits destroys enzymes and bacteria. Addition of large amounts of sugar provide an environment that will prevent bacterial multiplication. This concentration of sugar will draw water from bacteria and so they will die.	Soft fruits (e.g. strawberries, raspberries, oranges) can be used to make marmalade
Pickling and chutney making	pH Temperature	Initial boiling of fruits/vegetables when making chutney destroys enzymes and bacteria. Addition of a large amounts of vinegar to the ingredients reduces the pH value of the food causing bacteria to perish and be unable to multiply. Chutney is usually stored in glass jars which are heated before being filled to kill any micro-organisms which could contaminate the chutney.	Many vegetables and fruits can be used in chutney. Foods such as fish, eggs and onions can be pickled
Vacuum packing	Air Temperature	Vacuum products are also normally chilled to reduce temperature and so minimise bacterial multiplication. Oxygen is removed from the packaging of the product and so aerobic bacteria cannot multiply. These may or may not be cooked. If cooked, this process will kill many bacteria.	Many products such as meats e.g. bacon, salad leaves, cold meats

Table 4.8 Methods of food preservation

THE IMPORTANCE OF CLEANLINESS IN RELATION TO HEALTH

Example

This is a Credit level KU question relating to food preservation. It relies on you to recall and use your knowledge of food preservation. It is worth 3 marks; 1 mark for each explanation as to how each preservation method can extend the shelf life of food.

Remember that the question specifically asks how the method can extend the life of the food. This should be the central part of your explanation.

Explain how **each** of the following methods of home preservation extends the shelf life of food:

◆ freezing

◆ jam making

◆ vacuum packaging.

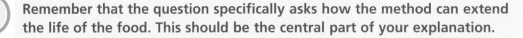

Sample answers:

Freezing

◆ *Temperatures of between minus 18°C and minus 24°C ensure that any bacteria in food become dormant and so cannot multiply thus preventing food spoilage.*

◆ *The process of freezing changes water to ice, therefore making water unavailable to bacteria. The bacteria cannot multiply thus preventing food spoilage.*

◆ *Some food products are blanched prior to freezing, thus killing some bacteria/enzymes. This reduces/stops their potential for food spoilage during storage.*

Jam making

◆ *The initial boiling of the fruit will kill bacteria/micro-organisms and so they cannot multiply, thus preventing food spoilage.*

◆ *The initial boiling of the fruit will kill enzymes and so prevents food spoilage during storage.*

◆ *The high concentration of sugar in the jam will reduce the potential of bacterial growth during storage due to its dehydrating effect.*

◆ *The containers are normally heat sterilised before use and this process kills any micro-organisms that cause food spoilage.*

Example *continued* ➤

Example *continued*

- ◆ *Jams are normally covered with a seal on the top during storage to prevent the development of mould growth on the jam, so extending shelf life.*

Vacuum packaging

- ◆ *Oxygen is removed from the packaging materials during this process and so most bacterial multiplication will be reduced, thus extending the shelf life of the food.*
- ◆ *Normally used in conjunction with chilling and so the low storage temperatures will slow down micro-organism multiplication, thus extending shelf life of the product.*

Food Poisoning

Key Words *and* **Definitions**

Pathogen: bacteria that can cause illness.

Perishable: food that spoils easily, like fruit, meat and fish.

It is estimated that as many as 5.5 million people in the UK suffer from food poisoning each year. But what is food poisoning?

Food poisoning is caused by harmful bacteria entering the digestive system. These bacteria, called pathogens, produce toxins that make us feel ill. The symptoms associated with harmful bacteria include

- ◆ stomach/abdominal pains
- ◆ diarrhoea
- ◆ vomiting
- ◆ nausea
- ◆ fever.

With food poisoning, all of these symptoms can last for several days.

The young, the elderly, sick people, babies, young children and pregnant women are all vulnerable to food poisoning. Special care needs to be taken when preparing and cooking food for these groups.

Cross Contamination of Food

Food poisoning is often caused by the transfer of harmful bacteria from one place to another. Bacteria are often transferred by vehicles. Common vehicles include:

◆ pets

◆ other animals

◆ humans

◆ equipment.

Figure 4.32

Here are some simple rules to follow when preparing foods that may contain harmful bacteria:

Keep raw and cooked food separate to prevent the transfer of bacteria. This relates to:

◆ Storage – in areas like refrigerators, store cooked foods above raw meat or fish to prevent the possibility of blood and fluids (which may contain harmful bacteria) dripping onto the cooked foods.

Figure 4.33

◆ Food preparation equipment – ensure that all equipment like chopping boards and knives are thoroughly cleaned with hot soapy water after/before use and use colour coded chopping boards for different food groups, e.g. red board for meat, green board for salad and fruit, etc.

Figure 4.34

Cover foods as much as possible to prevent transfer of bacteria by organisms such as flies.

Wash hands after handling high risk foods.

Clean work surfaces and equipment thoroughly before you start to prepare food and after they have been used with raw food.

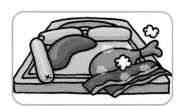

Figure 4.35

Preventing bacterial growth by controlling the temperature

The use of temperature is one way of controlling bacteria, as shown in the chart below.

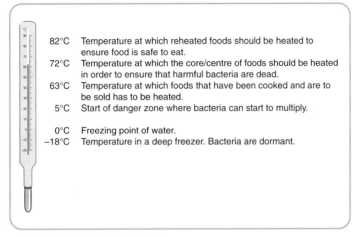

82°C	Temperature at which reheated foods should be heated to ensure food is safe to eat.
72°C	Temperature at which the core/centre of foods should be heated in order to ensure that harmful bacteria are dead.
63°C	Temperature at which foods that have been cooked and are to be sold has to be heated.
5°C	Start of danger zone where bacteria can start to multiply.
0°C	Freezing point of water.
−18°C	Temperature in a deep freezer. Bacteria are dormant.

Figure 4.36

Storing foods in the home

Storing foods correctly is important in preventing food spoilage and contamination. The following tips will be helpful in preventing food poisoning/spoilage:

◆ Perishable foods have a short shelf life and must be stored in a refrigerator or freezer in order to reduce the rate of spoilage. You will find out more about refrigeration and freezing later in this chapter.

◆ Non-perishable foods have a longer shelf life but must also be stored correctly to prevent contamination or spoilage.

◆ Dry foods should be kept in a cool, clean and dry area like a store cupboard.

◆ When using stored food, remember the golden rule: First in, First Out (FIFO). This means that you should always used the older foods first before they have the chance to spoil.

◆ When packing dried and tinned foods in a store cupboard, place the items with the nearest expiry date to the front of the shelf.

Refrigerators and Freezers

We have looked at the importance of temperature control in relation to food preservation and controlling bacterial growth. Refrigeration and freezing are two important parts of food storage that use the principle of temperature control to prevent bacterial growth. Let's look at each in turn.

Refrigerators

A refrigerator is used for the short term storage of perishable foods. As it has a working temperature of between 0° and 4°C, it slows down bacterial multiplication but cannot stop it. A refrigerator, however, can only work well if it is used correctly. Table 4.9 lists some simple rules that should always be followed when using a refrigerator.

Figure 4.37 A refrigerator

Rule	Reason
Refrigerators should be sited away from direct sources of heat and sunlight	to ensure that the working temperature does not increase above 4°C.
Ensure that the refrigerator is operating at a temperature below 5°C	to prevent bacterial multiplication.
Refrigerator should be kept clean and well ventilated	to prevent risk of cross contamination.
Foods should be stored in a refrigerator so that air can circulate	to allow cold air to circulate round food so reducing the core temperature of the food.
Raw foods like meat and fish should be stored below cooked foods	to prevent risk of cross contamination.
All food stored in the refrigerator should be covered	to prevent the risk of cross contamination and to prevent the food from drying out.
The refrigerator should be well maintained	to ensure that the refrigerator operates at correct temperature.
Food from open cans and containers should be transferred to covered containers before being stored in the refrigerator	to prevent the risk of cross contamination and also for safety reasons.
Ensure stock rotation in the fridge, removing all foods which have gone past the use by date	to minimise the risk of consuming food which may cause ill health.
Hot or warm foods should be cooled completely before being stored in the refrigerator	to prevent causing any increase in the internal temperature of the refrigerator which might result in bacterial growth in foods being stored.

Table 4.9

A refrigerator is generally used for the storage of non-frozen foods. However, some refrigerators have an ice box in which pre-frozen foods can be stored. This is because the temperature of the icebox drops below the freezing point and reduces bacterial growth significantly, but not completely. It is important that only pre-frozen foods are stored in an ice box as an ice box is not suitable for freezing fresh food.

A refrigerator ice box will have a star rating which gives you guidance as to how long pre-frozen food can be safely stored.

Star rating	Location	Temperature	Storage time
☆	Ice box	– 6°C	1 week for pre-frozen food only
☆☆	Ice box	– 12°C	1 month for pre-frozen food only
☆☆☆	Ice box	– 18°C	3 months for pre-frozen food only
★☆☆☆	Freezer	– 18°C or below	Long term storage of both pre-frozen and fresh foods

Table 4.10

Freezers

A freezer is used for both the short and long term storage of perishable foods. As it has a working temperature of –18°C, bacteria become dormant so multiplication is not possible. A freezer, however, can only work well if it is used correctly. Table 4.11 lists some simple rules that should be followed when using a freezer.

Figure 4.38 A freezer

Rule	Reason
All food for freezer storage should be well wrapped.	◆ To prevent the food from drying out. Freezing can remove the water content from the surface of unwrapped food, altering the quality of the food. This is known as freezer burn. ◆ All packing materials should be air and water tight.
Check your freezer is operating at the correct temperature.	◆ Freezer should be maintained at −18°C. Use a freezer thermometer to check. ◆ Modern freezers now have an built-in temperature indicator. ◆ Do not place hot or warm foods in the freezer to cool. This will raise the operating temperature of the freezer, making it less efficient.
Date mark and label all foods that you freeze.	◆ When frozen, it may be difficult to determine the contents of the food. ◆ Date mark the food to ensure you know how long the food has been stored.
Ensure good stock rotation in your freezer. Throw out all foods that have exceeded the recommended storage date.	◆ Foods should not be stored for longer than recommended, otherwise the quality of the food will deteriorate.
Do not over-pack your freezer.	◆ Cold air needs to circulate round stored foods to ensure effective freezing.
Do not refreeze food which has defrosted.	◆ Food which has thawed will have reached a temperature that allows bacterial multiplication to increase. ◆ Refreezing defrosted foods mean refreezing a larger number of bacteria!
When freezing fresh foods, use the quick freeze function if available.	◆ Many freezers have a quick freeze function – this reduces the operating temperature of the freezer to at least −26°C. ◆ This causes quicker freezing and smaller ice crystals to form inside foods. ◆ This helps to improve the texture of foods when defrosted.
Make sure that you freeze foods which are suitable for freezing.	◆ Not all foods are suitable for freezing such as fruits and vegetables with a high water content (tomatoes, cucumber, lettuce etc.). ◆ When freezing liquid based foods, remember that the volume of the liquid will increase. Make sure that you leave enough space in the storage container for this to happen (known as headroom).
Maintain your freezer on a regular basis.	◆ This will ensure that your freezer is working efficiently and effectively. ◆ Defrost your freezer on a regular basis – if you need to. Follow the manufacturer's instructions on how best to do this.

Table 4.11

Key Words *and* Definitions

Freezer burn: drying of the surface of frozen foods as a result of poor packing.

Quick freeze: ability to reduce the operating temperature of a freezer to –26°C in order to freeze foods quickly.

Questions *and* Answers

F In the Foundation paper from 2009 onwards, there will be a section of questions which are multiple choice. This means that you will be given a question and a series of answers. You simply have to choose the correct answer by placing a tick in the correct box. You can be asked about anything from the entire course content so you need to know your stuff!

Here is a range of multiple choice questions from this section. They will give you an idea of what to expect.

1   **What is the normal operating temperature for a refrigerator?**

    A   0°C to 4°C   ☐
    B   0°C to 8°C   ☐
    C   –5°C to –4°C   ☐
    D   5°C to 63°C   ☐

2   **What type of laundry instruction does the following symbol show:**

    A   washing   ☐
    B   drying   ☐
    C   dry cleaning   ☐
    D   ironing   ☐

Questions and Answers continued ➤

THE IMPORTANCE OF CLEANLINESS IN RELATION TO HEALTH

Questions and **Answers** continued

3 Select two micro-organisms from the following list:

A yeast ☐
B enzyme ☐
C mould ☐
D toxin ☐

4 Which of the following foods is most suitable for freezing:

A cucumber ☐
B lettuce ☐
C prawns ☐
D cheese ☐

5 What does the abbreviation FIFO stand for?

A Food Information for Ordering ☐
B First In First Out ☐
C First In First Ordered ☐
D Facts In Food Orders ☐

6 At what temperature should reheated food reach to endure food safety?

A 50°C ☐
B 63°C ☐
C 72°C ☐
D 82°C ☐

7 Why should you not over-pack your refrigerator?

A It makes it difficult to see the contents. ☐
B Air cannot circulate round the food to chill effectively. ☐
C It can crush the food. ☐
D There will be no space for other foods. ☐

8 On which shelf in a refrigerator should raw meat be stored?

A top shelf ☐
B salad drawer ☐
C bottom shelf ☐
D middle shelf ☐

Questions and **Answers** continued ➤

Questions and Answers continued

F | **Answers:**

1   A

2   B

3   A, C

4   C

5   B

6   D

7   B

8   C

You would get 1 mark for each correct answer.

When answering this type of question, start by eliminating those items that you know are not correct. This makes your final choice easier. If you don't know, make an educated guess – you may get it correct!

What you need to know!

Personal hygiene

Clothing care and laundry symbols

◆   washing
◆   dry cleaning
◆   ironing

◆   drying
◆   bleaching

Food safety and hygiene

◆   kitchen hygiene

◆   personal hygiene

Food spoilage

◆   bacteria
◆   yeasts

◆   moulds
◆   conditions for growth

Summary continued ➤

THE IMPORTANCE OF CLEANLINESS IN RELATION TO HEALTH

Summary *continued*

Preservation of food

- freezing
- jam making
- vacuum packing

- chilling
- pickling

Food poisoning

Cross contamination

Refrigerators and Freezers

THE IMPORTANCE OF SAFE PRACTICES IN THE USE OF RESOURCES AND MATERIALS

In the last chapter, we looked at food safety and ways of keeping a hygienic work area. In this chapter, we look at safe working practices in the home, not just in the kitchen. Here, we will identify common accident areas and how these could be prevented by looking at each section of the home and asking a few simple questions.

Key Words and Definitions

Burn: injury caused as a result of dry heat.

Scald: injury caused as a result of wet heat.

CORGI: Confederation of Registered Gas Installers. Always use a GORGI approved tradesman for all gas appliance fittings and repairs.

General Home Safety

It is important to check **gas** and **electric appliances/heaters** regularly in order to prevent suffocation due to a gas or carbon monoxide leak and to prevent electric shock.

Plugs, extension leads and sockets should also be in good working order to prevent electric shock or electrocution. Sockets should never be overloaded as this has the potential to cause a fire if the socket overheats.

You should never touch **electrical equipment** if your hands are wet because you could get an electric shock when the water penetrates the electrical equipment.

Children can be very inquisitive and it is important to keep **small items** such as coins and small toys out of reach. Toddlers and young children may put small items into their mouth and could choke on them if they swallow them. Small items left on the floor could also cause someone to trip over them and could cause an injury, including a serious fall.

When trying to reach **inaccessible places** or replacing light bulbs etc. you should use step ladders to help you reach. **Step ladders** are designed to be stable and support you when climbing and by using them you could help to prevent a fall. This is particularly important for the elderly who might not be stable on their feet.

Every house should have a first aid kit so that the inhabitants can respond quickly to any accidents.

Figure 5.1

Kitchen Safety

The kitchen can be a dangerous place, especially for children. Make sure that all **flexes** are out of the reach of children so that they do not accidentally cause themselves or others harm. A toddler might pull a flex and cause an item of equipment to fall, or may pull the flex and receive an electric shock. It is also important that items that contain **hot liquids** are kept out of reach to reduce the chance of burns and scalds. This includes **pots** and **pans** on the cooker top.

Figure 5.2 There are a lot of potential hazards in a domestic kitchen

When preparing food, always be sure you use appropriate protection for your hands and eyes. Use **oven gloves** when placing items into and removing items from the oven, and never put your face or hand over **hot oil** or other liquids.

Make certain that all the appliances in the kitchen area are in proper working order, and use them appropriately as described in their user manuals. **Gas appliances** should always be fitted and maintained by a CORGI registered fitter. They are specially trained in gas installation and repairs. Never assemble food preparation **equipment** like electric food processors if they are plugged into the mains, and certainly do not immerse any electric appliance into hot water to wash it, nor place it in a dishwasher.

If you keep **medicines** or **chemicals** such as bleach in the kitchen, be certain they are kept in a secure cabinet and out of reach of children. All dangerous medicines and chemicals should be stored in a **secure** place where children have no access. Chemicals should never be stored in containers designed for **fizzy drinks** because it is confusing for children and adults alike. Children are naturally curious and will not know if a product is dangerous.

If children are allowed to **help out** in the kitchen during cooking and eating times, make sure that they are properly supervised. Children should never be allowed to play in a kitchen by themselves because of the potential dangers that area presents.

Irons can also be a danger to children for similar reasons to those listed above. If left unaccompanied, a child may well pull the flex of the iron and this could cause a serious burn.

Sharp knives and scissors should always be kept out of reach of young people and stored safely. All sharp kitchen tools should be stored in a secure area to prevent children gaining access to them. A knife block or lockable drawer is an ideal storage place.

Young children who use high chairs should always be well secured to prevent falls. Make sure all harnesses are secured properly and that there are no worktops or other furniture within reach of the child. This helps to prevent the child from pulling themselves over or knocking onto them.

Wipe up all spills immediately to prevent falls, as well as for hygiene reasons.

When using a microwave oven, be sure that you use it in the manner it is intended. Do not attempt to fry food in a microwave oven, as there is a danger that the fat will catch fire. Never place metallic items in a microwave, including crockery with gold or silver decoration, as this will cause sparking and possible damage to the equipment.

Figure 5.3

If using cling film to cover containers in the microwave, use non-PVC cling film as this is specifically designed for microwave use. Also, remember that food cooked in a microwave oven can 'super heat'. This means that it can boil up suddenly and violently when moved or stirred. For this reason, always take care when removing foods from a microwave.

As with any electrical equipment, it is important that it is maintained properly. Clean the microwave oven regularly, especially the seal around the door. This reduces the possibility of any leakage. Additionally, ensure that your microwave is tested for leaks on a regular basis, usually yearly.

Living Room and Dining Room Safety

Fireplaces and wood stoves are common features of living and dining rooms. If your home has one, check that there is a fire guard protecting the gas, coal, wood or electric fire. This helps to prevent children from accidentally falling into the fire. It also prevents children having access to items that might start a fire.

Figure 5.4 A fire guard will help to prevent accidents in the home

Any furniture with **sharp edges** should have the corners protected. This includes brick fireplace hearths, bookcases and coffee tables. These edges and corners can cut and cause bruises easily if fallen against. You can buy **table corner protectors** to prevent such accidents.

As with hot liquids in the kitchen, make sure that **hot meals** and **drinks** are not left in reach of children. A child may accidentally knock over a hot meal or drink and cause themselves a burn or scald. Eat meals at the dining room table or always ensure that children are supervised.

If you use **tablecloths** on any tables, make sure that they do not hang over the table. This hanging fabric is easy for infants and toddlers to pull. If the cloth is pulled, the contents could fall on them and cause an injury.

Homes with **shiny** or **polished floors** often have small rugs on them. If your home has rugs, be sure that **slip guards** or **tape** are placed beneath them so that they don't accidentally slide when someone walks on them. The elderly or young, who might not be stable on their feet, could fall and be hurt if these aren't secured.

Hallways and Stairs

If there are young children in the house, **safety gates** should be fitted and used on all stairway areas. Safety gates prevent children from gaining access to the stairs and therefore help prevent accidents like falls.

All hallways and stairs should also be kept **free from clutter**. Stray toys and clutter can cause a person to lose balance when climbing stairs. This is particularly true of the young and elderly, who may be unstable on their feet.

Figure 5.5 Safety gates can help prevent accidents on the stairway

In areas where there are no windows, be sure that the **lighting** is adequate. This will ensure that people can clearly see the stairs and also allows people to see any clutter that may cause an accident.

On stairways, be sure the **bannister** is secure and maintained to prevent falls. The elderly and young in particular need a steady handle to support movement up and down the stairs to help with balance.

Bathroom Safety

Scalding is something always to be aware of in a bathroom, especially when running a **bath**. Always run the cold water before the hot to prevent anyone, especially toddlers, from being scalded should they fall into the bath.

Never leave children unattended during **bath time**. Given the dangers of being in water, bath times should always be supervised to prevent **drowning**.

Figure 5.6 The bathroom can be a dangerous place

To prevent falls in the bathroom, make sure there is a **non-slip mat** in the bath or shower. Baths and showers can have a slippery surface, especially when using soaps, shampoos and bath oils.

Never use **electrical appliances** in the bathroom. If water penetrates electrical equipment the result can be an electric shock or electrocution. Electric toothbrushes and beard trimmers should only be used with a grounded, appropriate socket.

Store **bathroom cleaners** in a secure cupboard to prevent accidental poisoning. All dangerous chemicals should be stored in a secure place where children have no access.

Chemicals should not be stored in containers designed for fizzy drinks because children are naturally curious and will not know if a product is dangerous.

Like kitchen knives, **razors** and **scissors** used in the bathroom should be kept out of sight and reach of young children. These items should be stored in a high position or a secure cupboard to prevent accidental cuts and wounds.

Bedroom Safety

Window locks should be fitted to prevent potential falls. This is particularly important if the bedroom is on a level above ground. Children are curious and may topple out of a window if it is able to be opened.

Figure 5.7 Blind cords should be kept out of the reach of children

Keep **blind** and **curtain cords** out of reach to prevent strangulation. A child may get the cord caught round its neck and cause injury or death. Secure cords in a place where the child has no access or cut the cord to remove loops.

Beauty products like **cosmetics** and **perfumes** should always be kept out of reach of children to prevent poisoning. As with kitchen and bathroom cleaners, all potentially dangerous chemicals or products need to be stored in a secure place where children have no access.

Garden and Outside Safety

All **fences** and **gates** should be secured to prevent accidents, especially if there are areas of water like pools and fish ponds nearby. This ensures that you know where the child is located and so keeps them safe.

Buckets or **containers** that might collect rain water should be removed from the garden to prevent drowning. A child can drown in even a small amount of water.

Figure 5.8 There are several safety aspects to consider in the garden

As with all **chemicals**, garden fertilisers and other products should be in correct, labelled containers and stored in a secure area. This will prevent accidental poisoning of children and pets, as well as making sure chemicals are not improperly mixed.

Fire Safety

Check that **smoke detectors** are fitted and checked regularly. In the event of a house fire, this will alert you and help to ensure a quick evacuation. These should be checked on a regular basis, especially if battery operated.

Keep **matches** and **lighters** out of sight and reach of children. Matches and lighters should be stored in a secure place so they are not accidentally used to cause a fire.

Be sure **plugs** are switched off at the socket and interior doors are closed before going to bed. A power surge could cause an electrical fire or electric shock.

Never **overload sockets**. Overloading may cause a power surge and potentially an electric shock or electric fire. Try not to use a power adaptor and certainly never overload it. Remember, also, to replace any flexes that are frayed, kinked or damaged. If handled incorrectly, a frayed flex can cause an electric shock.

Example

This is a 4 mark KU safety question from a General paper. It asks you to identify potential accidents and then to suggest a way in which the potential accident might be prevented.

Study **each** of the pictures below, which show accidents waiting to happen.

For **each** picture:

state **one** accident which could happen

explain how the accident could be prevented.

Figure 5.9 Picture 1

Figure 5.10 Picture 2

Sample answers:

Picture 1

Possible accident	Prevention
◆ Burn	◆ Pot handles should be turned in towards the side of the cooker.
◆ Scald	◆ Always ensure that frying pans are attended/adult is supervising the kitchen area.

1 mark for correct accident; 1 mark for correct prevention. Total 2 marks

Picture 2

Possible accident	Prevention
◆ Cut	◆ Knives should be stored in a knife block when not being used.
	◆ Knives should be removed to a safe area when not being used.
	◆ Knives should be stored in a secure area when not being used.
	◆ Knives should not be left lying unattended on a work surface.

Safety When Caring for Clothes

Even the most domestic chores require careful attention and precautions. When caring for clothing items, there are many thing you can do to protect yourself and your loved ones from being injured.

Figure 5.11

Washing machines and **dryers**, like other electrical appliances in the home, should be kept in good working order. This includes checking that **safety lock** features work properly. Children should be kept away from the machines when they are in operation and never allowed to play inside them. Do not leave a tumble drier, dishwasher or washing machine operating **overnight** or when you are out as they are a potential fire risk. The high wattage, friction and motors in the machines cause many home fires in Britain each year. Finally, do not **cover** or **obstruct** the vent of a tumble drier.

Irons require other precautions. If you are going to fill a steam iron with water, be certain it is **switched off** and **unplugge**d to avoid possible electrocution. Always set the iron to the **correct temperature** for the items you are ironing so that clothing is not damaged. If you need to leave the iron alone for a moment, make certain that the cord is **out of the reach of any children**. When you are done, leave the iron to **cool down** by placing it on its heel and making sure it cannot be knocked over or pulled down. **Fold** the ironing board and store away immediately after use.

Safety when sewing is another consideration when caring for clothes. **Store** all sharp tools such as **scissors** and **seam rippers** in a secure place out of the reach of children. When passing scissors to another person, **hold the blades closed** in the palm of your hand to allow the person receiving to take by the handle.

Figure 5.12

Never put **pins** or **needles** into your mouth, even for a few minutes. These items should be **stored** in a secure box to prevent accidental punctures, and any dropped pins or needles should be picked up at the end of a sewing session.

When using a **sewing machine**, concentrate on the task in hand – do not get distracted by other people or the television. Do not wear **loose fitting clothing** when sewing; this will prevent it getting caught in the machine. When done, **pack** all sewing equipment away, including the sewing machine which should have its needle at the lowest position. Take care when **lifting** the machine as it can be heavy and cause back strain. Regular **maintenance** of the sewing machine will ensure it works efficiently and safely.

Fat Fires

Figure 5.13

In the UK, about 20 people are killed each day as a result of fires that start in the kitchen. About 1/5 of these fires are the result of a chip pan or deep fat fryer.

Cooking fat can reach very high temperatures when used. Because of this, it is very difficult to control or put out a fire caused by burning cooking fat. Fat fires can be prevented, however, with some simple precautions. Never **fill** a chip pan more than 1/3 full to prevent splashes. Always **dry food** before immersing in the oil, if possible, because excess moisture will cause splattering and potential burns (remember, water and oil do not mix). If a chip pan is **smoking**, do not place any food into it because the fat is too hot. Finally, never leave a chip pan or a deep fat fryer **unattended**.

Should a fire occur even after you've taken these precautions, **do not try to move** the chip pan or fryer. Instead, when it is safe to do so, **turn off** the heat. If it is an electrical fire, **pull out the plug** or switch the electricity off at the mains. Next, place a fire blanket over the pan, or use a dry powder or carbon dioxide type fire extinguisher, to **suffocate** the fire. You can place a damp cloth over the pan if you do not have a fire blanket or extinguisher.

Do not pour water over the fire, as this will cause it to explode like a fireball.

Questions and Answers

F In some KU safety questions you may be expected to use your knowledge to answer questions that are not based on pictures or illustrations. Below is a 2 mark KU question from a Foundation paper.

List two safety rules to be followed when using a washing machine.

In this question, not only do you have to recall safety information, but you also need to make sure that the safety information you provide links to the use of a washing machine. This makes it a more complex question.

When thinking about this type of question, there are a number of general safety rules for the use of electrical appliances that you could use. In addition, there are some safety rules that are specific to using a washing machine. Both are shown in the following sample answer.

Questions and *Answers continued* ➤

Questions and Answers continued

F **Sample Answers:**

- *Never handle electrical appliances/switches/control buttons with wet hands.*
- *Washing machine should always be switched off at the mains supply before/after use.*
- *Do not use a washing machine if it has a damaged flex.*
- *Do not use a washing machine if it is damaged in any way.*
- *Ensure that the electrical plug has the correct fuse rating.*
- *Read the instruction manual if you are unsure how to use the washing machine.*
- *Do not leave detergents and other washing chemicals near the washing machine where children have access to them.*
- *Ensure that any safety lock features of the washing machine are working correctly.*
- *Ensure that young children do not have access to the washing machine whilst operational.*
- *Ensure that the washing machine door is always securely closed during washing/after unloading washing.*

Questions *and* Answers

C Safety can also be tested in HI questions. For example, in the question below you have to evaluate the suitability of a safety scheme for a given situation. This is a 3 mark HI question from a Credit paper; 1 mark is awarded for each point of evaluation.

Tom and Mandy Brown have a **two year old boy** and want to ensure **his safety**. Tom and Mandy live in a **second floor flat** and both are currently **out of work**.

Tom has read the following article in a local newspaper.

Do you have young children?

If so you will want to keep them safe. Each year many children are accidentally injured or killed in the home. At KIDS SAFE we have a scheme to help provide home safety equipment to families who have a low income.

We can provide:
Stairgates, fireguards, smoke detectors,
safety film for glass, window locks

The equipment is free, but there is a £10 fitting fee for each item of equipment borrowed. The equipment can be borrowed for a maximum of 12 months at a time.

Figure 5.14

Evaluate the suitability of the KID SAFE scheme for the Brown family.

In this question you are asked to evaluate the suitability of the scheme for the case study provided. The important parts of the case study have been highlighted. It is these that you need to refer back to in your answer.

Remember that in an evaluation question, your answers can relate to both the good and the bad points of the KID SAFE scheme, as long as you relate your answers back to the highlighted parts of the questions!

C

Sample answers:

◆ *The scheme is suitable for the Brown family as they have a young child whom they might want to protect from injury.*

◆ *The scheme is suitable for the Brown family as they are out of work and so may be on limited income and this scheme is designed for such families.*

Questions and Answers continued ➢

Questions and Answers *continued*

C

♦ *Although the family live in a second floor flat they may be able to use the stair gate to prevent access by children to the kitchen and so this may be useful.*

♦ *If the flat has central heating, the fireguard may not be of great value to the family.*

♦ *The smoke detector will be of benefit to the family as it would detect a possible fire/incident and so help to protect the family.*

♦ *The safety glass film may only be of value to the family if they have glass surfaces and so this item may not be useful.*

♦ *The window locks would be ideal for a family in a second floor flat with young children as it would prevent any child opening a window/falling from an open window.*

♦ *The £10 per item charge may limit the safety items that the family may want so making the scheme less effective.*

♦ *The equipment can only be borrowed for 1 year at a time making the scheme less effective as the items would have to be removed.*

Summary

What you need to know!

Procedures for the safe use of:

♦ Food preparation equipment   ♦ Laundering equipment.

♦ Sewing equipment

General home safety, specifically the following accidents and how to prevent them:

♦ Cut   ♦ Burn

♦ Scald   ♦ Fall

♦ Electric shock   ♦ Poisoning

DESIGN FEATURES

Design features are those parts of an item (equipment, clothing, cars etc.) that have been added in order to

◆ make the item work better

◆ make the item look better

◆ and/or add value to the item.

In this chapter, we will be looking at design features relating to two main groups:

Equipment:

Food preparation equipment e.g. food processors, knives, chopping boards

Sewing equipment

White goods – washing machines, tumble dryers, cookers and dish washers

Materials:

Food

Clothing

Footwear

Influences on Choice of Goods and Services

Before we look at specific examples in detail, there are some factors that we need to consider before we start shopping, and other factors that we should consider when making a final choice.

Income

The amount of money we have to buy goods will determine what we can buy. Generally, the more money you have the more choice you have. However, the most expensive choice may not always the right choice!

The amount of money you have influences choice in relation to:

◆ the types of foods you can buy – cheaper foods tend to be less nutritious, and often high in fat and sugar

◆ the type of shops that you buy foods in – lower income may limit you to shops that offer less well known brands at cheaper prices, like Aldi

◆ the variety you have – studies show that the less income a person has, the less food and less variety of food is eaten.

Sizing

We all have different shaped bodies and so if we are buying clothing, we need to think about our body size to make sure we buy clothing or footwear that fits. Likewise, if we are buying white or brown goods for the home, we need to consider their size to make sure that they fit in the space available.

Location

Depending on where we stay, how we buy our goods and services might be affected.

◆ If we stay in or near the city, then there are a wide variety of shops available for us.

◆ If we stay in a more suburban area, the access to a wide range of shops will be limited and prices may be higher.

◆ If we stay in a rural area we might prefer to shop by mail order or the Internet, where items are delivered direct to the home.

Other factors that influence choice include

◆ payment options

◆ advertising

◆ colour

◆ personal likes and dislikes

◆ style

◆ properties of the product, such as durability.

DESIGN FEATURES

Example

Let's think about a product and consider the influences that might affect your purchase.

Matt is a student who is going on holiday. He wants to buy a pair of swimming shorts. He has seen the following swim shorts on the Internet.

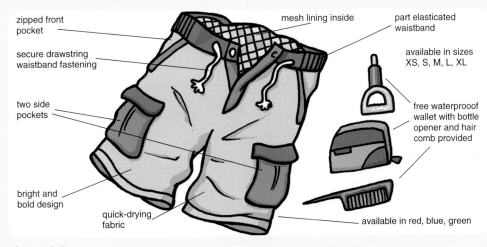

zipped front pocket

secure drawstring waistband fastening

two side pockets

bright and bold design

quick-drying fabric

mesh lining inside

part elasticated waistband

available in sizes XS, S, M, L, XL

free waterprooof wallet with bottle opener and hair comb provided

available in red, blue, green

Figure 6.7

All of the items noted above are design features. The person who has designed the shorts has added these features because they feel that these features would
◆ be important features for swim shorts
◆ help to sell the swim shorts
◆ make the swim shorts stand out from other shorts available.

It is up to each individual consumer to decide whether or not these features meet their particular needs or not. If you wanted yellow swim shorts, or swim shorts in an XXL (extra extra large) size, or ones that had secure side pockets, the shorts above would not be suitable for you!

Questions and Answers

There will usually be a design related KU question in the Foundation, General and Credit papers. In these questions you will normally be provided with an illustration of a product (food, textile or an item of equipment) which lists the design features. You would then normally be expected to give a reason for the suitability of the design for a particular situation.

Questions and *Answers* continued ➤

Questions and **Answers** *continued*

F Whilst this is an example from a Foundation paper, the same techniques should be used when answering similar questions from a General or Credit paper. This is a KU question worth 3 marks.

A student wants to buy a sandwich toaster which is safe, easy to use and easy to clean.

Study the design features of the sandwich toaster below.

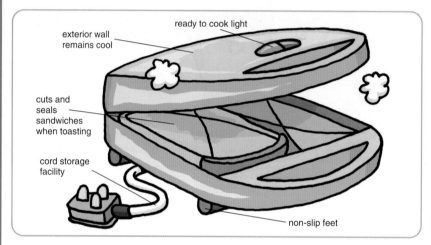

ready to cook light

exterior wall remains cool

cuts and seals sandwiches when toasting

cord storage facility

non-slip feet

Figure 6.8

Choose **three** of the design features shown.

State a reason why **each** design feature would be suitable for the student.

In this example, you have to select three out of the five design features given and explain why they would be suitable for the student. You are using your knowledge of design features to answer this question, remembering that you must relate your answer back to the case study provided.

When answering, choose your design features carefully. Select the ones that you feel confident about; that way you will get more marks!

You would be awarded 1 mark for each correct reason.

Sample answers:

Exterior wall remains cool

◆ *The exterior wall of the sandwich toaster will remain cool/will not get hot when operating and so this will not cause the student accidents/burns in use/will be safe to use.*

Questions and **Answers** *continued* ➤

Questions and Answers *continued*

- *If the exterior wall remains cool, this will make the toaster easier to use as there is no safety risk and so is meeting the student's needs.*
- *If the exterior wall remains cool, this will make it easy to clean after use as there is no safety risk and so is meeting the student's needs.*

Ready to cook light

- *The ready to cook light will indicate to the student when the toaster is ready to start cooking so making it easier to use.*
- *The ready to cook light will indicate to the student when the toaster is ready to start cooking, so it prevents any waste of ingredients as the student may be on a tight budget.*

Cord storage facility

- *The cord storage facility will mean that the toaster will not be a safety risk as there will be no trailing flex/cables during storage.*
- *The cord storage facility will mean that the product will not be easily pulled over so making it meet the safety needs of the student.*

Cuts and seals the sandwich when toasting

- *The toaster seals the sandwich when toasting, making it easier for the student to use – which is what the student wants.*
- *The toaster seals the sandwich when toasting and this will prevent excessive dripping from the sandwich filling onto/into the toaster so making cleaning easier for the student.*
- *The toaster cuts the sandwich when toasting, this saves the student having to cut the toasted sandwich with a sharp knife so making it safer.*

Non-slip feet

- *The toaster has non-slip feet and will not slip during operation so making it easier for the student to use.*
- *The toaster has non-slip feet which means that it will not slip when being cleaned so meeting the safety needs of the student.*

Design Features

There are many different aspects of design that a designer needs to consider:

- Aesthetics – how the products looks, feels, tastes, smells.
- Materials – what materials are used to make the product.

◆ Construction – how the product is made.

◆ Durability – how long the product might last.

◆ Safety – whether the product is safe to use.

◆ Performance – how well the product actually does what it is meant to do.

Look at these features in relation to equipment and materials shown in the following mental maps. Consider the positive and negatives of each design feature.

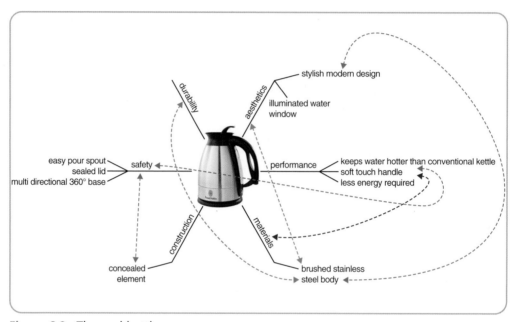

Figure 6.9 Thermal kettle

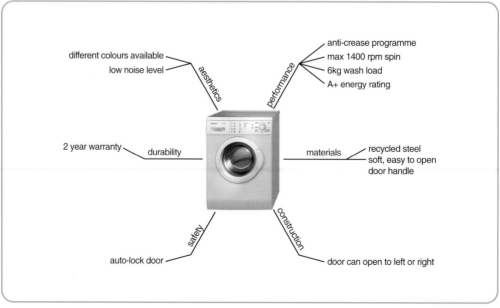

Figure 6.10 Washing machine

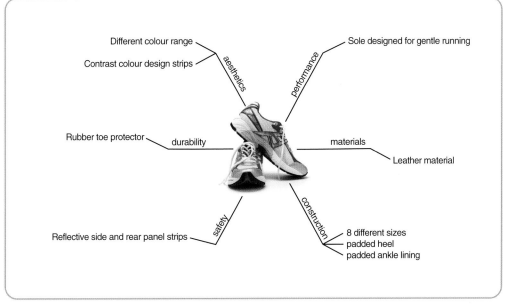

Different colour range — aesthetics

Contrast colour design strips — aesthetics

Sole designed for gentle running — performance

Rubber toe protector — durability

materials — Leather material

Reflective side and rear panel strips — safety

construction — 8 different sizes
padded heel
padded ankle lining

Figure 6.11   Trainers

Hints and Tips

It is a good idea to use mental maps not only when revising for your exams to see how much you remember, but also when planning your answers in an exam. However, don't spend too much time on the mental map because you will have to make sure you have time to write your response to each question!

Questions *and* Answers

Design features are an excellent source of content for HI questions. Again these will appear in all exam papers – irrespective of the level of the paper – and can relate to food items, textile items or electrical goods. Here is an example from a General level paper, worth 4 marks. This example uses a microwave oven as the theme for the question.

Tania is planning to buy a **microwave oven** for her **flat** which she will use mainly for **defrosting** and **reheating** foods.

The microwave oven should:

◆ be available in a **range of colours**

◆ be **easy to use**

◆ have a **power rating above 800 watts**

◆ have a facility for **grilling foods**.

Study the information about microwave ovens below.

Information about microwave ovens				
	Controls	Colours	Power rating	Features
A	touch	white	850 watts	◆ 9 power levels including defrost ◆ meal in one feature[1]
B	manual	white or silver	750 watts	◆ 6 power levels including defrost ◆ 30 minute timer
C	touch	white or silver	900 watts	◆ 6 power levels including defrost ◆ even cooking system[2]
D	touch	white, green, red, silver, blue	900 watts	◆ 8 power levels including express defrost[3] ◆ grill facility for browning foods

[1] can be programmed to cook at different power ratings and times to suit different recipes
[2] ensures that microwaves are evenly distributed inside the microwave oven
[3] defrosts up to 45% quicker than standard microwave ovens

State which microwave oven would be the **most suitable** for Tania?

Give three reasons for your choice.

Questions and Answers continued ➤

DESIGN FEATURES

Questions and *Answers* continued

G The starting point for this question is to highlight the important parts of the case study that you need to consider when selecting the correct microwave oven. This has been done in the example above.

The next stage is to use the criteria in the case study to eliminate possible choices:

◆ The microwave needs to have a power rating of above 800 watts. This automatically rules out choice B.

◆ The microwave oven needs to come in a range of colours. This automatically rules out choice A.

◆ The microwave needs to be able to grill, and the only information in the table relating to grilling is choice D.

So, by carrying out this simple activity of using the criteria to rule out poor choices, you can quickly come to the correct decision.

Remember that there will probably be two choices that are close, but only one that meets all the criteria.

G This means that you have selected D as the correct choice.

The next stage is to provide justification for your choice. To an extent, you have done this already by eliminating the other choices.

Sample answers:

Reasons for choice:

◆ *The microwave cooker has a facility for browning foods via a grill and Tania is looking for a microwave oven which has an option to grill foods.*

◆ *The grill facility may be able to be used by Tania to reheat certain types of foods and so meets her grilling requirement.*

◆ *The microwave oven comes in a range of colours and so will meet Tania's colour needs for her kitchen.*

◆ *The microwave oven has a 900 watt power rating which means that it will allow Tania to defrost/reheat food quicker than other models and this is what she is using the microwave oven for.*

◆ *The microwave oven has 8 power levels and should Tania wish to do more than defrost/reheat she will have the facilities to do so.*

◆ *The microwave oven has an express defrost facility which means that when Tania is defrosting food she will be able to do this quickly.*

◆ *The microwave oven has touch controls which will make it easy to use which is a requirement for Tania.*

Properties of Fibres

When buying textile items, it is important to consider what fibres have been used to make the item. In general, fibres are classified as being either natural or synthetic.

Natural fibres

These types of fibres are made from animals or plants. Common animal based fibres include wool (from sheep, goats and other animals) and silk (from the silk worm). Plant based fibres include cotton, linen and flax.

Key Words and Definitions

Drape: how the garment hangs or behaves when folded or pleated.

Durable: able to withstand wear and tear.

Breathable: allowing perspiration to evaporate, making clothes more comfortable to wear.

Lustre: the shininess of the fabric.

Biodegradable: able to decompose in soil.

Synthetic fibres

The term synthetic is most often used to refer to man-made fibres. These may be made from manufactured materials, or may be a mixture of natural and manufactured products.

Tables 6.2 and 6.3 detail some of the most common fibres used in textile manufacture. These are grouped into natural and synthetic fibres.

Fibre	Typically used for	Properties – Good points	Properties – Bad points
Cotton	towels sheets T shirts shirts/blouses underwear trousers	cool to wear absorbs moisture soft feel good drape durable can be washed and ironed easily	dries slowly creases easily
Silk	shirts ties dresses	warm to wear absorbs moisture soft feel good lustre good drape durable creases drop out	dry clean only can be expensive
Wool	jumpers suits dresses blankets	warm to wear absorbs moisture breathable soft feel durable	dries slowly can shrink careful washing or dry clean required may have coarse feel
Linen	table cloths suits dish towels	cool to wear absorbs moisture fast drying good drape durable can be washed and ironed	stiff feel creases easily and badly

Table 6.2   Uses and properties of common natural fibres

Fibre	Typically used for	Properties – Good points	Properties – Bad points
Viscose	blouses skirts	absorbent soft feel good drape can wash and iron	low warmth dries slowly not durable creases easily
Acrylic	blankets jumpers jackets	warm to wear non-absorbent fast drying soft feel good drape durable crease resistant easy care	not breathable
Nylon	shorts socks jackets	warm to wear absorbent breathable shower proof soft or coarse feel good drape durable creases drop out	dries slowly can shrink dry clean
Polyester	jackets raincoats baby clothing pyjamas	non-absorbent fast drying soft handle good drape very durable crease resistant easy care	low warmth

Table 6.3   Uses and properties of synthetic fibres

Commonly, textile items are made with more than one fibre, to combine the properties of each fibre. A blend of polyester and cotton is common. Polyester is easy to care for but does not provide warmth. Cotton provides warmth but is less easy to care for. Blending the two creates a relatively warm and easy to care for fabric.

However, with the developments in technology, new fibres have been developed that provide yet even more versatility and range of properties.

Microfibres

There are synthetic fibres that are very fine, about 60–100 times finer than a strand of hair. This gives textile items made from these fibres properties that are useful in outdoor clothing, such as sportswear. Two examples of microfibres that are commonly used in textile item manufacture today are Elastane and Tencel.

Elastane (commonly called Lycra) is typically blended with other fibres to make sportswear and tight fitting clothing. Its negative feature is that it offers little warmth. When blended, though, it offers

- a soft feel
- good drape
- durability
- crease resistance
- stretch
- easy care
- absorbency.

Tencel is a microfibre made from wood pulp that is frequently used for making shirts and jeans. Like Elastane, it offers little warmth but when blended, Tencel has many good features:

- a soft feel
- good drape
- breathable
- durable
- crease resistant
- easy to care for
- biodegradable
- absorbent.

Questions and Answers

The type of product and case study used in exam questions will vary greatly; however, the basic techniques for answering the questions will be the same. Here is a Credit level KU question worth 4 marks. This is based on a textile item – a backpack. The case study is more complex and there are more design features to consider.

Cameron is going on a **cycling trip** during the **summer holidays**. He wants to buy a **backpack** that he can **use on the trip** and for his daily **cycle to and from college**.

The cycle trip will last a **full day** with **one stop for lunch**. All cyclists have to bring their **own packed lunch** and **drinks** for the day.

Study the design features of the backpack shown below.

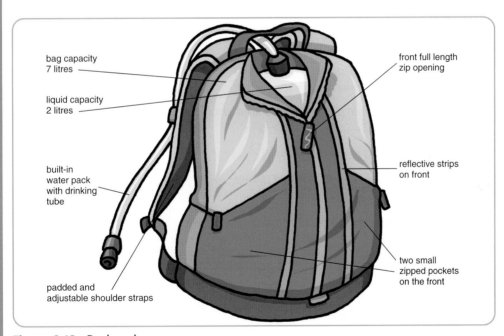

bag capacity
7 litres

liquid capacity
2 litres

built-in
water pack
with drinking
tube

padded and
adjustable shoulder straps

front full length
zip opening

reflective strips
on front

two small
zipped pockets
on the front

Figure 6.12 Backpack

Choose **four** design features and explain why each would meet Cameron's needs.

Remember to relate your answers back to Cameron and the highlighted parts of the case study.

Questions and Answers continued ➤

Questions and **Answers** continued

C | **Sample answers:**

Built in water pack with drinking tube

◆ *Saves having to carry an additional container within the backpack so saves space for other items.*

◆ *Ensures that Cameron will not forget to bring a drink container with him on the cycle.*

◆ *The cyclists have to bring their own drink and so Cameron can put his drink into this container.*

◆ *The built in water pack ensures that Cameron will have sufficient water to drink and he may get thirsty when cycling/may perspire a lot and need to replace this with water.*

◆ *The drinking tube means that Cameron will be able to drink the water easily without having to stop/without having to rummage in a bag for a water container.*

◆ *The drinking tube means that Cameron will be able to drink the water easily and so is more convenient when cycling.*

◆ *The liquid container is flexible and so it should not cause discomfort to Cameron when wearing/cycling/using.*

Two small zipped pockets on the front

◆ *Ideal for Cameron to place small items/cash/keys/mobile phone to be safe when he is cycling.*

◆ *Ideal for Cameron to place important items securely so they will not be lost curing the cycle.*

◆ *Having one pocket on each side means that the back pack should be balanced ensuring a safe cycle.*

◆ *As the pockets are on the front they will be easy for Cameron to access when he needs to get items from them.*

Front full length zip opening

◆ *Allows ease of access for Cameron when filling/emptying backpack.*

◆ *Allows Cameron to easily pack college books/cycling equipment/packed lunch for storage.*

◆ *The zip front means that items stored will be secure/not easy to lose.*

◆ *As the opening is on the front it will be easy for Cameron to access the inside of the backpack when he needs to get items from it.*

Questions and Answers continued

C | *Reflective strips on the front*

- *A good safety feature for Cameron if he has to cycle to college in the dark.*
- *Allows Cameron to be seen and so aid his safety on the road/when cycling.*
- *The strips are on the front and this means that they will be visible to motorists/other people when he is cycling.*

Padded and adjustable shoulder straps

- *The padded shoulders allow the backpack to be comfortable when worn/when cycling.*
- *The padded shoulders mean that the backpack will not dig into the shoulders when cycling/using.*
- *The shoulder straps are adjustable and so can be adjusted to make the bag comfortable in wear/when cycling.*
- *The shoulder straps are adjustable and so can be adjusted to suit the activity e.g. tighter when cycling.*

Bag capacity 7 litres

- *This capacity should be sufficient to allow Cameron to take his packed lunch and other items with him on his cycling trip.*
- *This capacity should be sufficient to allow Cameron to take materials to college and back.*

Liquid capacity 2 litres

- *This capacity should be sufficient to allow Cameron to take enough water to last his trip.*
- *As the cycling trip takes place in summer, Cameron will probably need this amount of liquid during his trip.*

You would use these same techniques whatever the product is – whether a food product, a textile product or an item of electrical equipment. Again, it is important that you select the design features that you feel confident about answering and remember to link each of your explanations as to the suitability of the design feature back to the case study provided.

Questions and Answers

Textile items also make good HI questions. The question below uses fibre properties as the theme for the question. However, this is a HI question and so you should be careful not to use information that you know about fabric properties that does not appear in either the case study or in the chart. Remember that this is a HI question and so all the information that you need will be contained within the question.

This is a 4 mark HI question from a General paper; 1 mark is awarded for the correct choice and a further 3 marks for the reasons for your choice.

A **local café** is buying **new trousers** for the **chef**. The trousers will be used **daily** and need to be **easy to care** for and **comfortable to wear**.

Study the information about trousers below.

Information about trousers			
	A	B	C
Fibre content	60% Polyester 40% Cotton	100% Cotton	100% Polyester
Absorbency	✱✱✱	✱✱✱✱	✱
Strength	✱✱✱✱	✱✱	✱✱✱
Stain resistance	✱✱✱✱	✱✱	✱✱✱
Laundering	✱✱✱✱	✱✱	✱✱✱
Sizes available	S,M,L,X,	S,M,L	One size fits all
Additional information	Flame resistant finish	Available in a range of pattern fabrics	Name can be printed on the trouser pocket

Key: ✱ Poor ✱✱✱✱ Excellent
S = Small M = Medium L = Large X = Extra Large

Table 6.3B Uses and properties of synthetic fibres

Select which trousers would be the **most suitable** for the chef? Explain your choice.

In the example, the important points from the case study have been highlighted in bold text. Use these criteria to start to eliminate poor choices.

The trousers need to be easy to care for. This relates to the following properties:

Ease of laundering – Choice A is the best

Stain resistance – Choice A is the best

Questions and **Answers** continued ➤

Questions and Answers *continued*

G The trousers need to be worn daily. This related to the following properties:

Ease of laundering – Choice A is the best

Stain resistance – Choice A is the best

Strength – Choice A is the best

The trousers need to be comfortable. This relates to the following properties:

Sizes available: Choice A has the biggest range of sizes to ensure comfort and a good fit.

Absorbency: Choice B is the best, with choice A second. However, in relation to the other requirements, Choice B would be an overall poor choice.

Therefore, by looking at some of the criteria we can see that the best choice would be A. You would next have to justify your choice.

Sample answers:

◆ *The chef will be working in a kitchen where hygiene is important and the excellent rating for laundering means that regular washing will not be an issue.*

! **Remember that if you are using information from a key within the chart, you need to use the correct terminology. If you had written 'good' rather than 'excellent' this would not have been accurate. The ✳✳✳✳ in the key relates to 'excellent'.**

G ◆ *The chef will be working in a kitchen where hygiene is important and the excellent rating for stain resistance means that clothing should be able to be cleaned easily/stains should not be difficult to remove.*

◆ *The chef will be working in a kitchen which can get warm so the ability to absorb sweat is important as this will keep the chef cool/comfortable and although these trousers do not have the best rating, the rating is still good.*

◆ *Chefs come in all shapes and sizes and this option comes in a range of sizes to ensure a good fit/comfortable to wear.*

◆ *The trousers have an excellent rating for strength and these may be subject to stretching, wear and tear associated with regular use in a kitchen.*

◆ *The trousers have an excellent rating for strength which is good as they are being used and laundered on a frequent basis.*

◆ *These trousers are flame resistant which is a good safety feature for a chef working in a café kitchen.*

HOW TO PASS STANDARD GRADE HOME ECONOMICS

Questions and Answers continued

The following answer would not be acceptable:

G

> *The fabric has 40% cotton content and this means that this fibre will be able to absorb moisture so making the trousers acceptable to the chef as they will be more comfortable to wear.*

The reason that it would not be accepted is that you are using your knowledge of the properties of cotton to answer this question – not the information provided on the chart or the case study!

Thinking About the Environment

The environment and recycling are big news:

'Stop wasting food' urges Prime Minister Brown (July 2008)

'Advisors to call on households to boost recycling' (July 2008)

'Mobile phone recycling a success' (April 2008)

Today, manufacturers make a big issue about the environment and make lots of claims about the products that they produce. When we buy goods and services, we need to think about the impact that our purchases might have on the environment.

There are two main areas that we should look at: household waste, including food and textiles, and our use of energy in the home.

Whatever we buy, there will always be a time when we need to think about disposing of the item. The environment should be a factor in this disposal.

Waste is what we dispose of because we no longer have a use for it.

When thinking about conservation of resources we should be thinking about the model of waste management shown on the right.

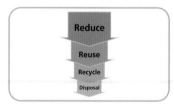

Figure 6.13

Reduce

Reducing means that you take positive steps to reduce the amount of waste produced. Table 6.4 shows how this can be done with material goods, such as food and clothing, while Table 6.5 shows ways of reducing the amount of energy your household consumes. By reducing our energy consumption, we help to prevent global warming.

What	How	Why
Avoid buying foods that have excess packaging.	Buy fruits and vegetables that are not pre packed.	Reduces waste packaging.
Compost at home.	Use a household composter or food digester.	Makes soil conditioner from food and gardening waste.
Repair goods.	Repair clothes and household items.	Makes goods last longer instead of being thrown away.
Use your own shopping bags.	Refuse any unnecessary shopping bags and use the bags that you have already.	Reduces waste from plastic.
Use solar power.	Buy appliances e.g. torches, calculators, that use solar power.	Reduces waste from batteries.

Table 6.4   Ways of reducing

Energy saving area	Potential saving per year (average)
Cavity wall or wall insulation will reduce energy loss through walls	£450 – £1400
Loft insulation will reduce energy loss through the roof	£130 – £450
Double glazing will reduce energy loss through the windows	£260
Draught proofing e.g. draught exclusion strips round internal doors	£60
Placing a jacket round the hot water tank	£50
Buy energy saving appliances – see pages 105–106	Can save up to £20 per year per appliance
Fit energy saving lights	£40
Turn off appliances and avoid placing appliances on stand-by	£30
Wash laundry at 30°C	£10
Turn off light after leaving a room	£10

Table 6.5   Ways to reduce energy usage

You would never be asked a specific question relating to the figures provided in this section; they are here to add interest and to let you see the extent of the waste issue and the scale of potential savings that can be made.

Other energy saving tips include:

◆ take a shower rather than a bath – it uses less water

◆ close curtains at night time to reduce heat loss through the widows

◆ keep lids on saucepans when cooking (when possible) as this speeds up the cooking process

◆ dry clothes outside (if possible) to avoid using a tumble dryer.

Reuse

Reusing involves the multiple use of an item, rather than disposing of it after one or two uses. This will not usually apply to food items because of obvious food safety issues. Look at the Table 6.6 for ways of reusing common household items.

What	How	Why
Reuse	Reuse scrap and wrapping paper	Avoids paper waste
	Reuse food containers and drinks bottles for storing food and packed lunches	Avoids packaging waste
	Reuse shopping bags or use cloth bags	Avoids waste from plastic bags
	Donate computers and mobile phones to be reused	Avoids electronic waste
	Donate textiles to charity shops or recycling centres	Avoids textile waste
	Zips, buttons etc. can be removed from clothes and reused. Fabric can be cut up and used for appliqué, patches	Avoids textile waste
	Donate or sell books, games, DVDs etc.	Avoids waste from unwanted goods
	Donate or sell furniture to be reused	Avoids waste from unwanted furniture
Recharge	Use rechargeable batteries	Avoids waste from batteries
Refill	Use refillable products e.g. fabric softeners, air fresheners	Avoids waste from packaging
Avoid disposables	Buy reusable alternatives e.g. real nappies rather than disposable	Avoids waste from single-use products
Buy recycled	Buy products made from recycled materials See the following page for more information	Saves resources needed to make new products

Table 6.6   Ways of reusing household items

Charity shops are a great place for reusing all sorts of items. Not only do they act as a centre for reusing goods, the funds that they raise go to good causes.

Recycle

Recycling is when waste material is used to make other products of an identical or similar nature. Most local authorities now have recycle points that can assist

Figure 6.14

with recycling. Likewise, most local authorities provide different forms of waste bins to allow us to recycle household waste.

There are many different products we use regularly that can be recycled:

Cans: These are made into new cans, car parts and building materials. Steel cans stick to a magnet. These are separated from aluminium cans at recycling points. Most cans are aluminium. Over 50% of all aluminium cans are recycled.

Food cartons: These can be turned into new paper products.

Glass: Glass can be made into new bottles or jars, concrete paving, golf course sand, as well as being used in art and craft products. Recycling one glass bottle can save enough energy to power your computer for 20 minutes!

Paper: This can be turned into new paper products like newspapers and toilet tissue. For every tonne of recycled newspaper we save 17 trees!

Plastic bottles: Plastics can be made into bin liners, compost bins, and even fleece jackets! It takes 25 two-litre plastic bottles to make one recycled fleece jacket!

Textiles: Clothing and fabric can be reused or turned into industrial cloth and new textiles. Over 70% of the world's population uses second-hand clothes!

Environmental labelling

Manufacturers now use a variety of different types of labels to provide information about energy conservation and recycling. When purchasing products, keep an eye out for as many of these labels as possible.

Other Regulations

The EU Energy Label is a compulsory notice that is applied to all white goods and home appliances sold within the EU. It allows the consumer to see the efficiency and energy consumption of a product.

The system consists of a series of letters from A to G for most appliances, but from A++ to G for refrigerators and freezers. A is the most efficient, while G is the least.

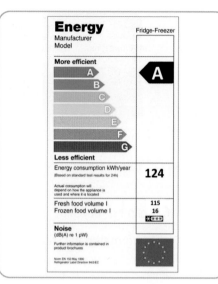

Figure 6.15a The EU energy label

The energy label on laundering machinery will indicate a rating for energy efficiency, wash efficiency and dry efficiency.

Figure 6.16

The most energy efficient products will display this logo:

Figure 6.15b The Energy Saving Recommended (ESR) label

In an examination paper you might be asked to identify particular features of white goods that make them energy efficient. Look at the following selection of appliances to see which features are common between different appliances, and which are unique.

Label	What it tells us
	This bottle should be recycled.
	This product is made from recycled aluminium/this product can be recycled.
	This product is made from recycled steel/this product can be recycled.
	This product is capable of being recycled.
	This product contains a percentage of recycled material. (The percentage will be indicated)
	Indicates that a fee has been paid for the recovery of the packaging in some European countries.
	This label indicates that this item of packaging should be carefully disposed/Do not litter.
	This label identifies the type of plastic used in the packaging to assist with labelling e.g. 3 means PVC has been used, 6 means Polystyrene has been used.

Table 6.7 Recycling labels and what they tell us

HOW TO PASS STANDARD GRADE HOME ECONOMICS

different sized rings or burners to suit different sized pans

smaller top oven can be used when cooking small portions of food

fan oven ensures quick and even cooking

half width grill allows only half the grill to operate when cooking small portions of food

Figure 6.17

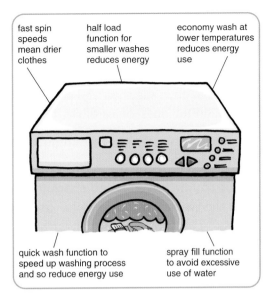

fast spin speeds mean drier clothes

half load function for smaller washes reduces energy

economy wash at lower temperatures reduces energy use

quick wash function to speed up washing process and so reduce energy use

spray fill function to avoid excessive use of water

Figure 6.18

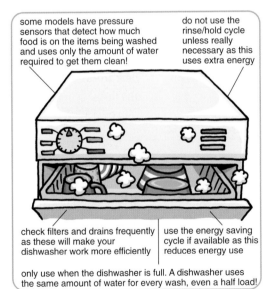

some models have pressure sensors that detect how much food is on the items being washed and uses only the amount of water required to get them clean!

do not use the rinse/hold cycle unless really necessary as this uses extra energy

check filters and drains frequently as these will make your dishwasher work more efficiently

use the energy saving cycle if available as this reduces energy use

only use when the dishwasher is full. A dishwasher uses the same amount of water for every wash, even a half load!

Figure 6.19

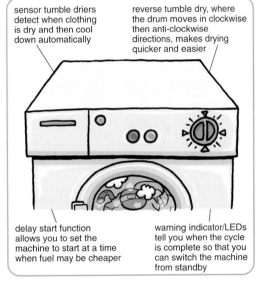

sensor tumble driers detect when clothing is dry and then cool down automatically

reverse tumble dry, where the drum moves in clockwise then anti-clockwise directions, makes drying quicker and easier

delay start function allows you to set the machine to start at a time when fuel may be cheaper

warning indicator/LEDs tell you when the cycle is complete so that you can switch the machine from standby

Figure 6.20

Hints and Tips
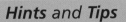

Some of these energy saving features can be found on more than one product, such as the LED or warning indicator. However, it is always a good idea to give a range of features if you are answering a question about two appliances. This is more likely to impress a marker than if you repeat the same feature twice!

HOW TO PASS STANDARD GRADE HOME ECONOMICS

Questions *and* Answers

Here is a Credit level HI question specifically about white goods. It has complex information in the chart and a lot of information in the case study, but by working through the question carefully, it is easy to select the correct answer!

A **busy** young couple with **limited income** are planning to buy a freezer for their **3rd floor flat**.

The couple have **limited space** in their kitchen. They plan to prepare meals at the weekend to **freeze for use during the week**. They like to **bulk buy food**. The couple often have **friends round for drinks**. The existing colour of the kitchen is **blue**.

State which freezer would be the **most suitable** for the couple?

Give **three** reasons for your choice.

Information about freezers			
	Freezer A	Freezer B	Freezer C
Type	Chest	Upright	Upright
Storage	1 freezer basket	5 removable and adjustable shelves	4 wire baskets with clear fronts
Freezing capacity	55 litres	90 litres	100 litres
Defrosting	Low frost feature[1]	Automatic defrost feature[2]	Low frost feature[1]
Fast freeze section[3]	No	Yes	Yes
Colours	White	Door panels available in most colours	White, Silver
Features	◆ Free ice scraper ◆ Free ice cube tray ◆ Free pizza freezing tray ◆ Free delivery to local areas	◆ Interior light ◆ Reversible door[4] ◆ In-door temperature indicator ◆ Integrated ice cube maker and dispenser ◆ Free delivery and installation	◆ Interior light ◆ Free ice cube tray ◆ Temperature rise indicator ◆ Free ice scraper ◆ £10 delivery charge
Energy rating	B	A	B

Key: Energy rating available from A to G
Energy rating A = most efficient   Energy rating G = least efficient
1 – reduced ice build up – no defrosting for 5 years.
2 – designed to minimise ice build up. No defrosting required.
3 – temperature reduced to allow for fast freezing of fresh foods.
4 – door can be positioned to open on right or left of the appliance.

Questions and Answers continued ➢

Questions *and* Answers *continued*

C So, how do you work your way through this question?

Start by highlighting all the important parts in the case study. This has been done above with bold text.

Next, use the highlighted criteria in the case study to start to eliminate some of the choices.

The couple are on a limited income so would be looking for the most efficient rated freezer. This is model B.

Their current kitchen colour scheme is blue. They might want a blue door panel for their freezer, so it matches. Model B comes with different coloured door panels.

The couple have limited space in their flat so a chest freezer would not be suitable. This rules out freezer A.

The couple buy food in bulk so need a large capacity. This rules out freezer A.

They have a third floor flat and so free delivery and installation might be useful. This rules out model C.

The couple are busy so would be looking for features that save time, like automatic defrost and easy to remove and adjust shelves.

All of this information points to model B. Look at the sample answers below and see how the information in the case study and the information in the chart have been matched together in the answers.

Sample answers:

◆ *Upright freezer may take up less space as it may be able to be put on top/under a work surface and so save space in a kitchen where space is limited.*

◆ *The freezer has lots of shelving and this would be good as it means that the couple can easily organise the large amounts of food that they plan to freeze.*

◆ *The freezer has adjustable shelving that means that any shape of container/food can be accommodated in the freezer as the couple do plan to use the freezer a lot.*

◆ *The shelving/adjustable shelving means that foods can be organised efficiently so that the couple can locate foods easily so saving time as this couple is busy.*

Questions and *Answers* *continued* ➣

Questions *and* **Answers** *continued*

C

- *The couple plan to store a lot of food in the freezer and this freezer can store 90 litres, which should meet their needs.*

- *This freezer has an automatic defrost function which mean that the couple do not have to defrost the freezer which is good as they are busy so saves them time.*

- *The automatic defrost function reduces ice build up in the freezer and so leaves more freezing space for all the bulk bought and home cooked foods that the couple plan to freeze.*

- *The fast freeze section reduces the freezing temperature for freezing of fresh foods and as this couple will be cooking meals during the weekend to use during the week, this feature is ideal.*

- *The fast freeze section reduces the freezing temperature for fresh foods and as this couple will be bulk buying foods, this feature is ideal if freezing non pre-frozen foods.*

- *This couple have a blue kitchen and the availability of different door panels in most colours means that they will be able to buy a freezer that matches their kitchen colour scheme.*

- *The freezer has an interior light that means foods can be located easily so saving time for the busy couple.*

- *The reversible door feature means that the freezer door opening can be selected on the right or left hand side and so this gives more flexibility in a kitchen where space is limited.*

- *The in-door temperature indicator means that the couple will be able to monitor and check the freezer temperature easily so saving this busy couple time.*

- *The in-door temperature indicator means that the couple do not have to buy a temperature guide separately and this is good as the couple are on a limited income.*

- *The integrated ice maker and dispenser is ideal for the couple as they entertain friends for drinks regularly and so this feature means ice on demand for drinks.*

- *The integrated ice maker and dispenser is ideal for the couple as it means they do not have to think about spending time making ice cubes and they are a couple with limited time.*

Questions *and* **Answers** *continued* ➤

Questions and Answers *continued*

C
◆ *The free delivery/installation of the freezer is ideal for the couple as they are on a limited income and so this will save them having to spend additional money on delivery and installation.*

◆ *The free delivery/installation is ideal for the couple as they live in the 3rd floor flat and so this will save them time and effort which is ideal as they are a busy couple.*

! **Remember that in this type of question you are asked to justify your choice of item/product. You are not asked to justify your rejection of the other models.**

Summary

What you need to know!

Influences on choice of goods and services:

◆ Food   ◆ Clothing
◆ Footwear   ◆ Food preparation equipment
◆ Sewing equipment   ◆ White goods

Design features:

◆ Materials   ◆ Construction
◆ Performance   ◆ Safety
◆ Durability   ◆ Aesthetic properties

Properties of fibres

◆ Natural   ◆ Synthetic

Conservation of resources

◆ Energy efficiency   ◆ Labelling
◆ Recycling, reusing, reducing

THE PHYSICAL NEEDS OF INDIVIDUALS AND FAMILIES

We have looked at how designers create products to anticipate our needs, as well as to help companies make profit. However, every individual has their own specific needs and every family is different in terms of structure, income and expenditure.

In this section of the book we will examine the physical needs of individuals and families in relation to:

◆ general wellbeing

◆ clothing

◆ obtaining consumer advice

◆ the rights and responsibilities of the consumer

◆ product labelling.

Key Words *and* Definitions

Wellbeing: a state of happiness, good health and prosperity.

General Wellbeing

What is wellbeing? In this section of the chapter we are going to look specifically at factors that will affect your health such as sleep, exercise, personal hygiene and substance abuse.

Getting enough sleep

It is a natural fact of life: we need to sleep in order to

◆ allow the body to rest

◆ allow the body to grow and develop

◆ help the body to break down food and use it for growth, repair and maintenance

◆ help us perform during the day

◆ be in a good 'mood'.

Figure 7.1

When we are asleep, our body does not shut down. It still needs to produce hormones, pump blood around the body, and perform other functions – just not at the rate that is required during the day.

So what can we do to try to get enough sleep to help our body to work well?

◆ Regular exercise can help us sleep – but don't exercise too near to bed time.

◆ Avoid having TVs, computers etc. in your bedroom, all of which can discourage sleep.

◆ Try to avoid alcohol or caffeine (found in cola, tea and coffee) before going to bed.

◆ Try not to eat too much before going to bed – your stomach needs some rest time as well.

◆ A well ventilated bedroom can help you sleep.

◆ A warm bed might help. Going into a cold bed may well waken you up and make you feel more alert.

Exercise

When you exercise, you do not just feel fitter; your general wellbeing improves. But why else is exercise important?

Exercise makes you feel:

◆ less tired

◆ less stressed

◆ more happy.

It also:

◆ helps to reduce your weight because you will burn up energy

◆ exercises your body muscles and organs, such as the heart

Figure 7.2

◆ keeps joints, tendons etc. healthy, which helps to avoid injury

◆ regulates your appetite

◆ helps you to sleep

◆ can reduce the risk of certain diseases and conditions like heart disease, stroke, some types of cancer and osteoporosis.

It is important to seek medical advice before starting an exercise programme if you are overweight or suffering from a medical condition.

Personal cleanliness

After exercise, we need to have a shower or bath to remove any perspiration. We should also be washing, showering or having a bath daily. As we go about our daily activities, our body picks up grease, grime and dirt. We also naturally perspire, or sweat. If this sweat is not removed, it can act as an ideal food for bacteria. The end result is that our bodies begin to smell – otherwise known as body odour, or BO.

This cleanliness also applies to our hair, which should be washed on a regular basis. Additionally, we should be brushing our teeth at least twice a day to remove any food deposits which can lead to dental decay.

Substance abuse

Substance abuse is when a person takes an excess of any substance – alcohol, cigarettes, drugs, solvents etc. – to such an extent that they become 'hooked' on them, or they use them to become 'high' or get a 'kick'.

Let's look in turn at each of the major substances abused by people:

Alcohol

Excess alcohol consumption can lead to a variety of problems. Some of the most common are:

- depression
- heart failure
- mental health issues

- liver cirrhosis (severe liver damage)
- damage to the brain and nervous system
- damage to relationships, finances and career.

Remember – you need to be over 18 to buy alcohol. In some places, including some supermarkets, the age for buying alcohol has been raised to 21.

Smoking

Tobacco is a known carcinogen, or cancer-causing substance.

Smoking can lead to problems like:

- gum disease and bad breath
- cold and flu
- high blood pressure

- coughs and shortness of breath
- mouth ulcers
- asthma.

Over time it can lead to many serious problems like:

- stroke
- bronchitis
- bladder cancer

- mouth and throat cancer
- lung cancer
- infertility

- heart disease
- stomach ulcers
- death.

THE PHYSICAL NEEDS OF INDIVIDUALS AND FAMILIES

Drugs

Illegal drugs are those that are not controlled or supervised by medical professionals. These drugs include substances such as:

- heroin
- ecstasy (E)
- magic mushrooms
- cannabis
- cocaine/crack
- LSD
- amphetamines/speed
- anabolic steroids.

These drugs are not prescribed and, if caught in possession of these drugs, you can be sent to prison for a long time. If this is not bad enough, there are serious side effects of taking illegal drugs including:

- lung disease and cancer e.g. through smoking cannabis
- lack of motivation and mental health issues e.g. through smoking cannabis
- heart attack or fitting e.g. through taking cocaine
- panic attacks e.g. through taking cocaine
- liver, kidney and heart attacks e.g. through taking ecstasy
- death e.g. through taking ecstasy, heroin
- hallucinations e.g. through taking LSD or magic mushrooms
- depression and mental health issues e.g. through taking speed
- HIV, Hepatitis through sharing infected needles.

People who are addicted to drugs, either legal or illegal, should seek urgent medical help.

Solvent abuse

We know that illegal drugs such as heroin and ecstasy can cause death. However, did you know that cigarette lighter fuel, solvent based glues, hairspray and deodorant aerosols can also cause death?

These products, with about another 30 common household products, can be used to get a 'high' by sniffing the gases contained within the product. As with drug abuse, solvent abuse has serious health risks, including drowsiness, confusion, aggressiveness, heart attacks and even death.

People who are addicted to solvents or use them to get a 'high' should seek urgent medical help.

HOW TO PASS STANDARD GRADE HOME ECONOMICS

Questions *and* Answers

Questions about general well being are common in all exam papers. They can be KU or HI questions.

The following is a HI question related to general wellbeing. It uses an electric toothbrush as the context for the question. This is a General question worth 4 marks; 1 mark for the correct choice and 3 marks for justifying your choice.

Parents are buying their **teenage student son** an **electric toothbrush** as part of his birthday present.

The toothbrush should:

◆ **encourage regular and correct tooth brushing**

◆ **remove plaque** from teeth

◆ be **rechargeable**

◆ **reduce teeth staining**

◆ **last for a long time.**

> You should brush your teeth twice a day ensuring all teeth are cleaned.

> It should take 2 minutes each time you brush your teeth.

Study the information about electric toothbrushes below.

Information about toothbrushes			
	A	B	C
Power source	Battery	Rechargeable battery	Rechargeable battery
Plaque removal	95% removal	90% removal	95% removal
Storage case	Yes – fabric	No	Yes – hard plastic
Features	◆ Protection cap for toothbrush head is included ◆ Pressure sensor activates if too much pressure is applied ◆ Removes some stains	◆ Safe for use with braces ◆ Includes one free tube of toothpaste ◆ Smart-timer helps to ensure two minutes brushing time	◆ Side by side brush movement ◆ Indicator showing length of time spent brushing ◆ Reduces staining in 28 days
Guarantee	3 years	2 years	3 years

State which electric toothbrush would be the **most suitable** for the student?

Give three reasons for your choice.

Questions and *Answers continued* ➢

Questions *and* Answers *continued*

G The first step in this type of question is to read the case study carefully. In this case, the case study is about parents wishing to buy an electric toothbrush for their son. The case study provides you with the specific requirements for the toothbrush. It is these requirements that you need to use to select the most suitable toothbrush. To do this you should start by highlighting the important points in the case study. This has been done for you.

You then need to study the information about each toothbrush carefully. At this point use the highlighted requirements to start to decide which toothbrushes are not suitable. For example:

> The toothbrush needs to be rechargeable. This rules out toothbrush A.

> The toothbrush needs to remove plaque. Toothbrushes A and C have the best plaque removal percentage.

> The toothbrush needs to last. Toothbrushes A and C have the longest guarantee.

Already we have narrowed the best choice to toothbrush C. However, there are other reasons to select toothbrush C.

Sample answers:

♦ *The parents want the toothbrush to be rechargeable and this option has a rechargeable battery so is meeting their needs.*

♦ *The parents want the toothbrush to remove plaque and this toothbrush removes 95% of plaque so is meeting their needs.*

♦ *The toothbrush should last the student for a long time and this toothbrush has a hard plastic storage case so protecting it from damage/helping to extend life so meeting his needs.*

♦ *The toothbrush should encourage the student to undertake regular and correct tooth brushing technique and this brush provides side by side brush movement so ensuring an effective clean so meeting his needs.*

♦ *The toothbrush should encourage regular and correct tooth brushing technique and this brush provides an indicator of how long you have spent brushing your teeth so ensuring a 2 minute clean can be achieved.*

♦ *The toothbrush should last the student for a long time and this toothbrush has a three year guarantee in case it breaks down so meeting his needs.*

♦ *The parents want the tooth brush to reduce staining and this model promises to reduce staining in 28 days so meeting their needs.*

Clothing Needs

As individuals, we all have different body shapes and sizes and different likes and dislikes. However, when buying clothing for different groups in society, there are a number of factors that we need to consider.

In this section of the book we will be looking at the factors that might need to be considered when buying clothing for all age groups and abilities.

Why do we wear clothing?

- to **protect** our body from the environment – from wind, rain, sun and snow
- to avoid **offending** or **distracting** other people who are uncomfortable with nudity
- for **identification** purposes e.g. school uniform to identify the school you attend
- for **safety** reasons e.g. firemen wear clothing that protects them from heat/fire
- for **legal** reasons, because you would be arrested if you were to walk the streets of your town or city naked!
- to express our **individuality**, **creativity** or **membership** of a group.

Babies

For this section of the chapter we are considering babies to be under the age of 1 year old. There are a number of elements that will impact what a baby should wear, as illustrated below:

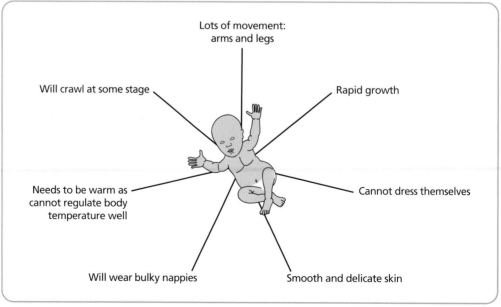

Figure 7.4

Bearing these development features in mind, Table 7.2 indicates the types of factors that you might wish to consider when buying clothes for a baby.

Factor	Explanation
Fastenings	Should enable clothing to be removed or put on easily. Velcro or poppers are ideal on babygrows for ease of opening or closing.
Easy to wash	Baby may be sick on clothing or there may be leakage from the nappy. Clothing needs to be washed on a regular basis and so should be easy to wash.
Easy to dry	Clothing needs to be washed on a regular basis and should be quick to dry so it can be used again if needed.
Easy to iron	Caring for a baby can be time consuming. Clothing should be easy to iron for this reason.
Absorbent	Baby will sweat and so to ensure comfort, clothing should be able to absorb sweat.
Non irritant	Babies have delicate sensitive skin and so clothing should be comfortable to wear against the skin to prevent irritation. Zips, buttons etc. should be positioned so as not to cause discomfort.
Durable	Clothing should be able to withstand wear and tear of stretching, crawling, rubbing. Should be able to withstand regular laundering.
Safety	No ties or ribbons that might strangle a baby, cause injury if fingers, toes etc. get caught. Flameproof to ensure safety.
Insulating	Babies have problems controlling body temperature and so clothing should keep babies warm in cold weather, keep babies cool in warm weather. Natural fibres e.g. cotton or layering clothing will help to maintain warmth. Short sleeve tops and short leg bottoms are ideal for warmer months.
Stretchy	Clothing should not restrict movement either in design or in fabric properties. Knitted fabrics for babygrows are ideal for this purpose. Stretchy fabrics allow for ease of dressing which can be difficult with active babies.
Fibres	Cotton and cotton blends are ideal because of their properties.

Table 7.2

Toddler

For this section of the chapter we are considering toddlers to be between the ages of 1 and 3 years old. There are a number of factors that will impact what a toddler should wear, as illustrated on the following page:

Bearing these development features in mind, Table 7.3 indicates the types of factors that you might wish to consider when buying clothes for a toddler.

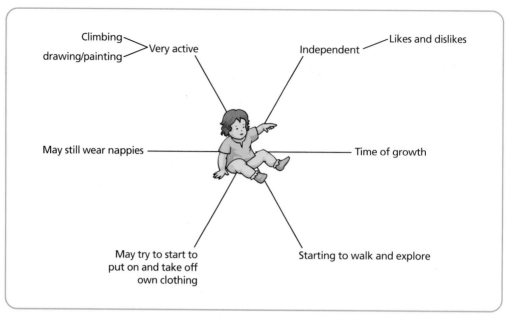

Climbing — drawing/painting — Very active   Independent — Likes and dislikes

May still wear nappies — Time of growth

May try to start to put on and take off own clothing   Starting to walk and explore

Figure 7.5

Factor	Explanation
Fastenings	Should enable clothing to be removed or put on easily. Velcro, studs or large buttons are ideal as they can help a toddler to do/undo own clothing. Elasticised waistband is ideal to assist the child to put on and take off own trousers/skirt.
Easy to wash	Clothing needs to be washed on a regular basis due to the activities that a toddler may be involved in and so should be easy to wash.
Easy to dry	Clothing needs to be washed on a regular basis and should be quick to dry so it can be used again if needed.
Easy to iron	Toddler may get dirty often and so clothing needs laundering often. Clothing should be easy to iron for this reason.
Absorbent	Toddler may be active and will sweat, so to ensure comfort clothing should be able to absorb sweat.
Durable	Clothing should be able to withstand wear and tear of stretching, running, climbing etc. Should be able to withstand regular laundering.
Safety	Nightwear should be flameproof. Neckties should be avoided to prevent strangulation. Baggy clothing may catch on items and cause injury.
Stretchy	Clothing should not restrict movement either in design or in fabric properties. Stretchy fabrics allow for ease of dressing which can be difficult with active toddlers.
Protection	Toddlers will be active and will explore. Clothing with padded knees, elbows will help prevent injury and may also help with durability.
Aesthetics	Toddler will start to develop likes and dislikes e.g. colours and this should be reflected in the clothing purchased.

Table 7.3

When buying shoes for a toddler, there are two golden rules to keep in mind: toddlers should have their feet measured each time a pair of shoes is bought to ensure they are the correct fit, and Velcro fastened shoes are good for encouraging a child to dress him/her self.

Teenagers

Most teenagers will have their own idea of what they want to wear, their likes and dislikes, and so the factors that need to be considered are different from other age groups.

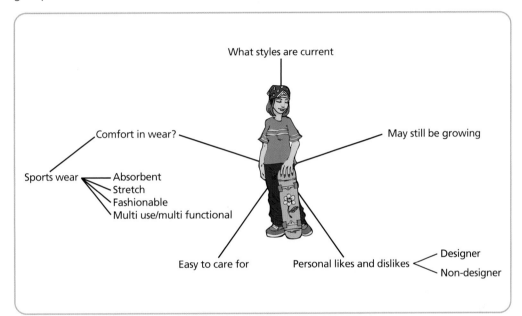

Figure 7.6

Factor	Explanation
Designer label	Some teenagers will buy for the 'label' rather than actual functionality. Some will not buy designer labels in preference for 'non branded/designer' goods.
Safety	No sharp buckles etc. that may cause injury.
Easy to launder	May have a lack of time or interest in laundering. May not have knowledge/skill to launder. Dry cleaning can be expensive. May wear item a lot and so needs to be easy and quick to clean.
Cost	Available budget may determine what can be chosen.
Beliefs/tradition/culture	Some religions/cultures have specific rules about clothing and these may affect purchases.
Peer group pressure	Teenagers may be influenced by what their friends wear. Teenager may buy clothing that makes them feel part of a bigger group.

Table 7.4

HOW TO PASS STANDARD GRADE HOME ECONOMICS

Bearing in mind the development features in Figure 7.6, Table 7.4 indicates the types of factors that you might wish to consider when buying clothes for a teenager.

Adults

There are no particular factors that are specific to adults. All of the general factors that link to other groups will apply, such as likes and dislikes, size and cost. There may be additional considerations, though, if there has to be a uniform or suit for work.

Elderly

Elderly people often have demands for clothing that are unique. Their mobility and living environment will impact on what they should wear, as illustrated below.

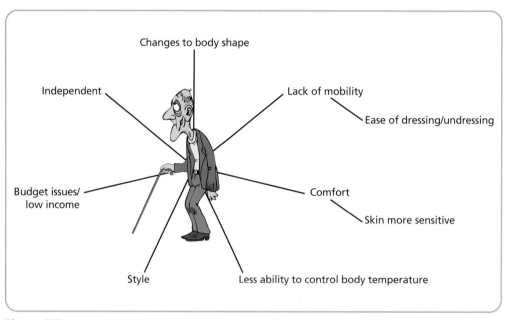

Figure 7.7

Bearing in mind these development features, Table 7.5 indicates the types of factors that you might wish to consider when buying clothes for an elderly person.

Hints and Tips

Remember that the elderly are not always frail, with walking sticks, false teeth and little money. They can be active, healthy and have money to spend. Try not to make these assumptions when answering KU questions.

If you are answering a HI question about the elderly, remember that your answer must relate back to the information provided about the elderly person in the case study.

Factor	Explanation
Fastenings	To assist with the putting on and removing clothing, fastenings need to be easy to use and handle e.g. Velcro, larger buttons, press studs.
Elasticated waistbands	Due to restrictions in movement, an elasticised waistband may help to ease putting on and removing clothing. This will also make clothing comfortable and perhaps extend wear as it can still fit even if a small amount of extra weight is gained.
Easy to wash	Clothing should be easy to care for as the elderly may not have ability or inclination to undertake a lot of washing.
Easy to dry	Clothing should be easy to dry as the elderly person may not have a tumble drier.
Easy to iron	Clothing should be easy to iron due to possible mobility difficulties/arthritis of hands making ironing difficult.
Absorbent	Clothing should be able to absorb sweat in order to ensure comfort.
Durable	Clothing should withstand wear and tear to ensure value for money.
Safety	Clothing needs to ensure safety. Clothing which is too long or baggy might catch and cause an accident. Clothing should be lightweight so as to aid movement.
Stretchy	Clothes which have stretch would help with dressing and ease of movement.
Protection	Protection for the cold is important to the elderly. Natural fibres, knitted and fleece products and layering of clothing will help with warmth, particularly in winter months. Elderly can be prone to hypothermia.

Table 7.5

Key Words and Definitions

Hypothermia: condition where the body temperature reduces quickly to below 35°C. This can be fatal.

Pregnant women

Women who are pregnant have special concerns that affect not only their comfort, but also the comfort and safety of the child they are carrying. There are a number factors that will impact what they should wear, as illustrated on the following page.

Bearing these development features in mind, Table 7.6 indicates the types of factors that you might wish to consider when buying clothes for a pregnant woman.

Good shoes are very important for pregnant women. Shoes should be comfortable and supportive, as they will have to support extra weight. Also, pregnant woman sometimes suffer from swollen ankles and this will limit the type of shoes that can be worn. Flat and sensible is the motto!

HOW TO PASS STANDARD GRADE HOME ECONOMICS

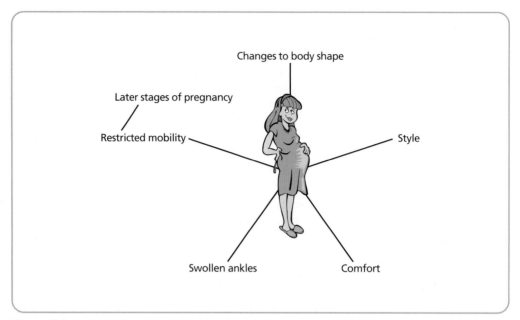

Figure 7.8

Factor	Explanation
Fastenings	Because of an expanding tummy, a pregnant woman should consider clothing that is loose fitting and with an elasticised waistband. The position of buttons and other fastenings should be considered in relation to comfort when wearing. Position and type of fastening should also be considered in relation to ease of use as when in later stages of pregnancy mobility may be an issue. Fastenings should be adjustable, if possible, to accommodate growth.
Loose fitting	To allow for ease of movement and also to allow for growth of the tummy during pregnancy.
Fibres	Natural fibres will help to absorb moisture so aiding comfort. Maternity clothing usually contains Lycra or Spandex to provide 'stretch' so aiding comfort and movement. Should be soft and non-irritant, or non-itchy, which would make you feel uncomfortable.
Openings	If breastfeeding, mothers-to-be should consider buying nursing clothing. This is clothing which has been designed with openings on items like blouses and dresses to make the process of breastfeeding easier.

Table 7.6

Hints and Tips

When given a question about choosing clothing for a specific group, think about the following questions:

1   Is there anything that will affect their ability to put on or remove clothing? If yes then look out for features like suitable fastenings and stretch fabrics e.g. lycra, knitted.

2   Are there particular needs like being warm or cool? If yes, then think about:
    ◆   fabric properties: knitted, fleece and layering traps air so insulates and keeps warm, while cotton absorbs moisture to keep you cool
    ◆   design features: short sleeves to keep you cool, long sleeves to keep you warm
    ◆   fabric finishes: treated to make showerproof, waterproof.

3   Are there particular needs to keep items like keys safe? If yes, then consider zipped pockets or other suitable fastenings.

4   Are there particular safety requirements? If yes, then consider:
    ◆   reflective or fluorescent strips/fabric
    ◆   fabric treated to make flame resistant
    ◆   safe fastenings, such as no ties round neck.

5   Are there any specific aesthetic features that are required?
    ◆   Colour, size, style
    ◆   Does the item need to travel well in a suitcase? In this case, you would look for crease resistance, easy to iron.

6   Is there a specific budget that needs to be taken into account?

Example

G   The individual needs of a group will often appear as HI questions in exam papers. Here is an example with sample answers. Look carefully at how the answers relate back to both the information provided in the case study and the information provided about each product/item.

Parents want to buy a new single duvet cover for their 6 year old daughter, Emma.

Both parents work all day and like to **spend the evening with Emma.**

Example continued ➢

Example continued

G Emma likes **dancing** and recently had her bedroom painted in **bright colours**.

Study the information about duvets below.

Information about duvets			
	A	B	C
Colours available	dark blue, black, brown, white	red, blue, yellow, green, pink	white, black, cream
Designs available	flowers, hearts	ballet dancer, butterflies	cartoon characters
Laundering information	warm iron machine wash	little or no ironing required machine wash	iron when damp machine wash
Additional information	Only available in double bed size	Matching pillowcase included	Matching pillowcase available to buy

State which duvet would be the **most suitable** for Emma's parents to buy?

Give three reasons for your choice.

You would be awarded 1 mark for the correct choice and 3 marks for providing reasons for your choice.

Note: the important points in the case study have been highlighted for you.

Sample answer:

*Correct choice: Duvet **B***

Reason for choice:

◆ *The duvet is available in a range of colours/bright colours and so should match in with the recently decorated bedroom.*

◆ *The duvet comes in ballet dancer design and this should appeal to Emma who likes dancing.*

◆ *The duvet requires little or no ironing and this would appeal to the busy parents as it means less work for them when they come home/means they can spend more time with Emma/can spend more time with Emma rather than spending time ironing.*

Example continued ➤

Example continued

G

◆ *The duvet is machine washable and this is good as it means it can be washed easily so saving the busy parents time/so saving the parents time which means they have more time to spend with Emma/so the parents' evenings are not spent washing.*

◆ *A matching pillowcase is included with the duvet and so will complete/match the newly decorated bedroom.*

Remember to write your answers in such a way that you link back to the information provided in the case study and the information provided about the item/product.

Clothing, textile items and safety

Textiles in the home can be exposed to different types of fire hazards. Cigarettes and matches are the two main causes of textile fires in the home, particularly bedding and upholstered furniture like sofa beds, arm chairs and mattresses. There are a variety of different labels available for products with textiles, each indicating the extent to which the product meets flammability regulations.

Figure 7.9

Children's nightwear is also another possible source of danger as it has the potential to catch fire quickly and easily. Children and the elderly are the most vulnerable groups. There are now mandatory and voluntary measures in place to control the fire performance of fabrics used in nightwear.

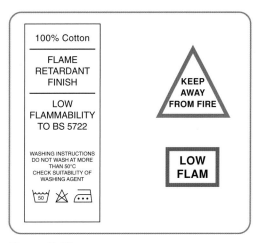

Figure 7.10

THE PHYSICAL NEEDS OF INDIVIDUALS AND FAMILIES

These regulations ensure that, in particular, nightwear for children

◆ does not exceed maximum size measurements for the age group

◆ satisfies flammability tests (BS 5722).

All new furniture and products that are subject to these regulations must also carry a permanent label.

Adult nightwear, pyjamas and bathrobes do not have to meet the flammability test but they must have a permanent label which indicates whether or not the item has had the flammability test, similar to ones shown above.

Hints and Tips

In an exam paper, you would probably be provided with a picture of one of the labels and asked to explain what protection this label gave to the consumer.

Obtaining consumer advice

In this chapter, we have already looked at rules and regulations that cover clothing and textile items. There are, however, other forms of rules and regulations (laws) that are there to protect the consumer from dangerous goods and services and 'dodgy' traders.

You will need to know the name of each item of law and the main ways in which it protects the consumer. You should know at least four points of protections linked to each Act of Parliament. Note: you should try to remember the name of the updated regulations.

Sale and Supply of Goods Act 1994

This act was updated in 2002 by the **Sale and Supply of Goods to Consumers Regulations**. If you buy goods from a trader (e.g. shop) the goods that you buy must be:

1 of satisfactory quality. This means that the goods should be of a standard expected, taking into account factors like price and description of the goods.

2 fit for the purpose made known to the seller. For example, that a CD player plays CDs, that a hand held camcorder records home videos.

3 as described. A short sleeved shirt should have short sleeves; Scottish salmon should be Scottish!

So what happens if you buy goods and any of the terms above are broken? You are entitled to one of the following:

1 A full refund. This means that you should return the goods to the retailer as soon as the fault is known and within a reasonable time.

2   A repair or a replacement. You have the right to ask for a repair or a replacement providing it does not cost more than you paid for the item.

3   A reasonable amount of compensation. If you have accepted the goods and after a reasonable amount of time it becomes faulty, you may be able to get a repair. However, if the fault cannot be put right you may be entitled to compensation, which may not be the full value as you have already had use out of the product.

Remember you have no rights if you were told about faults or defects before purchase, made a mistake when purchasing the item, or change your mind.

Trade Descriptions Act 1968 and 1972

This act was recently updated by the **Consumer Protection for Unfair Trading Regulations 2008**. Most of the Trade Descriptions Act has now been repealed (withdrawn), but the protection that it provided is covered in the new 2008 Regulations.

Under the Trade Descriptions Act it is an offence for a trader to make false statements about goods offered for sale, for example, a trophy being labelled as silver when in fact it is stainless steel. This also applies to services.

The 2008 Regulations were introduced as a result of decisions taken at the European Parliament. The aim is to ensure fair trading across Europe and prevent different countries having different regulations relating to misleading trade and marketing. If you buy goods from a trader in Spain and the marketing of the goods is 'misleading', you will be protected by the same Regulations that would apply in Scotland.

The Consumer Protection Act 1987

This act was also recently updated by the **Consumer Protection for Unfair Trading Regulations 2008** (see above). Major sections of this 1987 Act have now been repealed, but the protection that it provided is covered in the new 2008 Regulations.

The Consumer Protection Act ensures that, where a person is injured or dies as a result of using defective consumer goods, compensation can be claimed. The Act established a general safety requirement for all consumer goods in the UK. The Act also gives the government and local authorities the power to suspend the sale or importation of goods that may cause a danger to public health.

This Act protects the consumer from traders who give misleading price indications to consumers. An example of this is a business that makes cameras advertising nationally using the line 'Digital cameras for £5', knowing that they have a very small number of such cameras available at that price and that when the stock runs out consumers may then opt for a more expensive option.

Food Safety Act 1990

This is a wide ranging Act that affects everyone involved in the food industry. The Act applies to all food premises and ensures that food must:

1 be of the nature, substance and quality demanded, including content and origination.

2 not be falsely or misleadingly described, such as making a false claim about a food product.

3 not have been rendered injurious to health, like adding something to the food that may cause an injury to the consumer.

If a trader can show that he has taken all reasonable steps to prevent any food safety incident, then he may not be prosecuted.

The Food Hygiene (Scotland) Regulations 2006

These Regulations were updated in 2007 by **The Food Hygiene (Scotland) Amendment Regulations 2007**. These rules apply to all businesses which prepare, handle or sell food. The Regulations try to ensure that all businesses involved in food production operate in a safe and hygienic manner. They specifically state that:

1 all food businesses must be registered

2 premises should be kept clean and properly equipped in relation to:

- ◆ Premises
- ◆ Equipment
- ◆ Food handlers
- ◆ Washing facilities
- ◆ Services
- ◆ Practices
- ◆ Transport

3 food must be handled hygienically

4 staff must be appropriately supervised or trained

5 if staff are ill, they must report this to a supervisor and, if necessary, be removed from the food preparation area

6 all parts of the food production process must be assessed to try to minimise hygiene issues

7 the temperature of the products must be controlled.

Hints and Tips

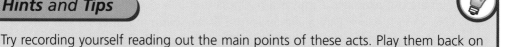

Try recording yourself reading out the main points of these acts. Play them back on your iPod or MP3 player as you walk to school, cycle, or take part in other activities.

Example

Let's look at two different types of questions that you might get asked in an exam about consumer law.

Explain two ways in which the Trade Descriptions Act 1968 and 1972 can protect the consumer when buying goods and services.

This is a 2 mark Credit KU question specifically about an Act. You need to recall your knowledge; 1 mark is given for each correct explanation.

Sample answer:

This act makes it an offence if a trader:

- *applies a false trade description to any goods*
- *makes certain kinds of false statements about the provision of services, accommodation or facilities.*

Here is another example:

Mary has bought a compact disc player.

Explain three ways in which the Sale and Supply of Goods Act 1994 will protect Mary when purchasing the compact disc player.

This is a three mark Credit KU question specifically about an Act. You need to recall your knowledge; 1 mark for each correct explanation.

Sample answer:

- *The Act states that products must be of satisfactory quality when purchased and so if the product does not work correctly Mary will be entitled to a refund.*
- *The Act states that the product must be as described (orally or in writing) and so if the product does match this description, Mary will be entitled to a refund.*
- *The Act states that the product must be fit for the purpose intended and so if the product does not play compact discs/does not perform a function expected of a CD player then Mary will be entitled to a refund.*
- *Depending on the circumstances, such as the amount of time lapsed, Mary may be entitled to a repair or refund instead.*

Hints and Tips

You need to be able to recall information about legislation so you need to know it all. Spend 10 minutes a night reading the main points of each Act.

Although we have looked at some of the legislation that is in place to protect the consumer, it is not always possible to remember or recall all this information when we face problems with goods or services that we buy. However, there are a number of organisations available who can assist consumers should they need help. Let's look at some of these.

Citizens Advice Bureau

The Citizens Advice Bureau (CAB) offers free, confidential and independent advice to the general public. CAB can be found in most towns and cities and operate as charities.

CAB provides advice covering a wide range of areas, including debt, housing, benefit, employment and immigration, legal situations and consumer buying.

This is a very reliable organisation that offers advice to people on an individual basis.

Consumers' Association

The Consumers' Association is a registered charity in the UK that trades under the name of 'Which?'. It offers independent advice to consumers via a subscription. Their magazine, *Which?*, offers consumer advice in a range of areas, including reviews of consumer products and services, product information and specifications, and 'best buys' on product groups. Approximately 700,000 people subscribe to *Which? Magazine*. Which? also publishes a wide range of books.

In addition to product advice, Which? campaigns on behalf of the consumer on a range of issues. This is a very reliable organisation that offers advice to those individuals that subscribe to the service. Which? does not handle specific issues and problems from individuals, but deals with issues that relate to larger groups of people.

Consumer Advice Centres

Some local authorities operate Consumer Advice Centres. These offer a range of functions similar to CAB and are a very reliable way to offer advice to individual people.

Consumer Direct is a government funded, online and telephone based service which offers a range of clear and practical consumer advice. This service can help both before and after you buy, as well as providing information relating to goods and services, your rights and consumer issues. This is a very reliable organisation that offers individual advice to people.

Many manufacturers also have Consumer Advice Centres, providing information to consumers about the range of products that the manufacturer sells. These tend to be online or telephone based services. You need to be careful when seeking advice from this type of advice centre as they are not independent and the advice might not always be impartial.

Departments of Consumer Protection, Trading Standards and Environmental Health

These are local authority-organised bodies which are there to enforce consumer protection laws. As well as being 'enforcement' officers, these departments may also offer advice to individual consumers. Different local authorities have different names for the functions that they offer.

Consumer Protection and Trading Standards departments enforce consumer legislation, offer help and advice regarding topics like debt or issues with a purchase, assist traders to comply with relevant legislation and investigate rogue traders, bringing action to traders where necessary.

The Environmental Health Department ensures a cleaner, safer and healthier place to live and work. Specific services usually include enforcing consumer legislation, specifically those relating to food safety and hygiene, addressing health and safety issues, pollution control and public health protection.

These different bodies offer free, independent and reliable advice to individual consumers.

Example

F Here is a Foundation level HI question linked to organisations that protect the consumer. It is worth 3 marks. You simply have to indicate which organisation would be best suited to help with each of the situations provided.

Read the information about consumer organisations below.

Consumer Organisation A	Consumer Organisation B	Consumer Organisation C
Protects the consumer from food which is not fit to eat. Inspects food shops and restaurants to make sure they are hygienic.	Offers advice on what is the best product to buy. Produces books and magazines containing information about consumer rights.	Provides help with filling in forms and applications. Offers advice on debt prevention.

State which consumer organisation would provide the most suitable advice in each of the following situations:

Example continued ➤

THE PHYSICAL NEEDS OF INDIVIDUALS AND FAMILIES

> **Example** *continued*
>
> F
>
> **Situation 1:** A consumer needs to complete a passport application form.
>
> **Situation 2:** A consumer has bought bread which is mouldy.
>
> **Situation 3:** A consumer wants to buy a new washing machine.

Situation 1 matches to organisation C because it mentions help with filling out forms.

Situation 2 matches to organisation A because it mentions food that is unfit to eat.

Situation 3 matches to organisation B because it mentions advice about the best buy.

Product labelling

As well as legislation and consumer bodies, there is product labelling that can assist consumers to make good choices. The charts and illustrations below show the mandatory (legal) and voluntary labelling that is associate with consumer products.

Food Labelling

The illustration below shows you the information that has to be provided by law.

Product name or description of the product
Should describe in a clear way what the product actually is. In this case a 'creamy parsley sauce'.

Additional ingredients
If additional ingredients are required to make the product, these must be listed. In this case you also need milk and butter.

Preparation instructions
If required, the product must provide instruction on how to prepare or use.

Cooking instructions
If required, the product must provide instruction on how to cook.

Figure 7.11a

Ingredients list
Listed in descending order of weight. The ingredient which is biggest in weight is listed first – in this case Wheat Flour.

Date marking
Products should have an indication of durability – how long they will last. If perishable (last for a very short time) a 'Use by date' must be provided. If the food will last for a medium to long term, a 'Best Before' date will be provided. (See page 139 for more information.)

Product weight
The weight of the product must be provided. This can be a metric measure e.g. 25g or a number, e.g. 6 sponge cakes. The 'e' symbol means 'average' weight, in this case 26g.

Origin of product
The place of origin of the product must be provided; in this case the UK.

Name, address of manufacturer, seller or packer
To allow contact to be made with the producer.

Storage instructions
If the product requires specific storage instructions they must be provided.

Figure 7.11b

The following information is provided on the sample label but is not mandatory:

◆ Serving suggestion – provides an idea as to how this product might be served.

◆ Nutritional information – this is not mandatory, but if it is provided it must follow specific guidance. If a product makes specific claims, like being low in salt, then it must support that claim with nutritional labelling information.

◆ Hints and tips – useful serving idea for the consumer.

◆ Bar code information – see below.

◆ 'Suitable for vegetarians' information – see below.

Additional product labelling information

The following types of labels may also be found on products:

Label	Type of product	Notes
	Wild-caught sea food and wild-caught sea food products.	Shows that the fish have been caught from an independently-certified sustainable and well-managed fishery. Fish with the MSC logo can be traced back to the sustainable fishery that caught them. (www.msc.org).

Label	Type of product	Notes
	Organic foods e.g. fruit, vegetables, meat.	Organic food is produced from a natural and sustainable system of agriculture which avoids the use of pesticides and prohibits synthetic fertilisers and GM ingredients. The Soil Association organic symbol is the UK's largest and most recognisable trademark for organic produce. Wherever you see it you can be sure that the food you have purchased has been produced and processed to strict animal welfare and environmental standards.
	All microwave ovens and products which can be cooked in a microwave oven carry this symbol. The important information is the information in the top right and bottom right boxes.	The top right number – in this case 700 W, tells you the wattage of the microwave oven. The bottom right letter will range from A to E, each letter indicates how quickly this oven can heat up a small portion of food. All food products which can be microwave cooked will have these symbols on the packing. These help you to determine how long you should cook the portion of food to ensure food safety.

Remember, when heating food in any appliance, heat it until it is piping hot. It is crucial to kill off any bacteria that may be on or in the food item.

Label	Type of product	Notes
	The label of the British Toy and Hobby Association, called the Lion Mark. Found on toys.	Shows that the toy or item has been made to meet quality and safety standards of the Association. Members of the Association supply about 95% of all toys sold in the UK.
CE	The European Union CE mark. Displayed on a range of goods e.g. toys, low voltage electrical goods.	Means that products displaying this label meet essential requirements of the relevant European health, safety and environmental protection legislation.
INTERTEK BEAB Approved	The mark of the British Electrotechnical Approval Board. Found on all small electrical appliances designed for the home or the office.	The label indicates that this electrical product has been independently evaluated as a product made to the highest European and international standards for safety.
	The registered trademark of the British Standards Institution. This is known as the Kitemark and is found on goods and services ranging from fire extinguishers and smoke alarms to garage services and doors and windows.	This is a voluntary scheme based on organisations applying to have their products and/or services tested to standards set down by industry representative and BSI. The scheme provides a labelling (certification) service that ensures the products or services meet the required standards and are safe and reliable.

This is the double insulation symbol that is found on electrical appliances which have been designed in such a way that they do not require a safety connection to electrical earth. This reduces the potential of receiving an electrical shock from the product.

The Eco-label is an EU label that helps you to select products that have been designed with the environment in mind. Found on products such as home appliances, cleaning materials, mattresses, office supplies, gardening and Do It Yourself products.

Products awarded this logo meet EU standards covering all aspects of product life from production to disposal.

This is the logo of the Confederation of Registered Gas Installers.

CORGI is the UK body that has responsibility for the registration of tradesmen who are trained in gas installation. When looking to have a gas appliance installed in your home, look out for a tradesman who is CORGI registered. This ensures that the person is trained and competent in gas installation.

This is the symbol of the Vegetarian Society, a group (charity) that promotes vegetarianism. This symbol is shown on foods (and in cafés and restaurants) that meet the standards of the Society.

This is the trademark logo for the Vegan Society, an organisation that promotes the benefits of veganism. Products bearing this logo are suitable for vegans and have been registered with The Vegan Society.

The symbols shown on the following page are designed to control substances which are hazardous to health and so protect people from ill health caused by exposure to hazardous substances. The symbols are easy to recognise. They are generally found on chemicals like cleaning products.

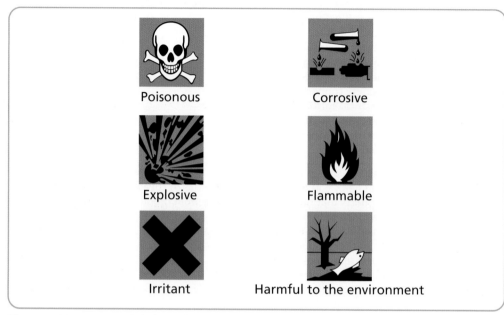

Figure 7.24 Warning labels and their meanings

Increasingly, you will find this label on food packaging. This is an attempt to encourage consumers to buy food which is healthy to eat. The label provides information about the amount of fat, saturated fat, sugar and salt in a food product. It uses a traffic symbol rating system. If the product has a high amount of any of these nutrients it will have a red

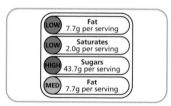

Figure 7.25

light – indicating that the product may not be a healthy choice. This system allows you to compare similar products and so select the one that is the most healthy.

However, as with all food labelling, it is not always that easy. Not all food manufacturers have adopted this scheme. Some have adopted another scheme which is shown below.

The GDA (Guideline Daily Amounts) system is based on the label providing information about how much a particular food product will contribute to the recommended daily intake of different nutrients. In this case, the label tells us how the amount of salt, sugars, fat etc. are in the product and how this contributes to your advised daily intake. This product contains 0.2 g

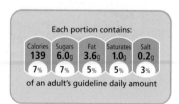

Figure 7.26

salt and this would account for 3% of your recommended daily intake.

Most packaged foods are required to be date marked with an indication of the minimum durability of the food – how long food will last. There are two main types of date marks: Use by and Best before.

Use by marks are applied to foods which are highly perishable and are likely to be a possible danger to human health after a short period, such as fresh meat, fish, poultry, cooked meat, paté, dairy products, ready made meals, salads and soft cheeses. They are required to be marked with 'a day' and 'a month', e.g. Use by 28 January.

Best before marks are applied to foods which will have a shelf life of three months or less, like bread or hard cheeses. They are required to be marked with 'a day' and 'a month', e.g. Best before 04 March. Packers may add a year to either of the above should they wish to do so, e.g. Use by 29 January 2005.

'Best before' may also be applied to foods with a shelf life of between three months and 18 months, provided it is marked with 'a day', 'a month' and 'a year'.

Best before end marks should be used on foods intended to have a shelf life in excess of three months, such as frozen and tinned foods. They are required to be marked with 'a month' and 'a year'. Alternatively, for products with a shelf life of over 18 months, this indication may be in the form of a year only, e.g. Best Before End 2007.

Example

The following information is found on the label of a packet of cheese.

Explain why **each** item of information would be important to a consumer.

Item of information 1

Item of information 2

Item of information 3

This is a three mark KU question from a General paper. It is asking you to recall your knowledge of food labelling.

Sample answers include:

Item of information 1

◆ *Indicates the date by which the food should be consumed.*

◆ *Indicates the date by which the food should be consumed to remain safe to eat.*

◆ *Indicates that the food is perishable and should be eaten by the specified date.*

◆ *Indicates the date by which any food already purchased/stored should be disposed.*

Example continued

G

Item of information 2

◆ *Indicates to the consumer that food must be stored at a cool temperature/stored in refrigerated conditions/stored at below 5°C.*

◆ *Indicates to the consumer that in order for the food to remain fresh it should be refrigerated/chilled.*

◆ *Indicates to the consumer that food will only keep to its 'use by' date if the storage instruction is followed.*

Item of information 3

◆ *Indicates to the buyer that the container/packaging will contain approximately 300 grams of food.*

◆ *The e symbol indicates that an approximate weight is given for this product/it may contain slightly more or slightly less than 300g.*

1 mark would be awarded for each correct explanation.

Summary

What you need to know!

Choosing clothing for different groups of people:

◆ Babies

◆ Toddlers

◆ Teenagers

◆ Adults

◆ Elderly

◆ Other special groups

Choice of clothing:

◆ Protection

◆ Comfort

◆ Suitability

◆ Safety

Product labelling

General Wellbeing

Organisations that help the consumer:

◆ Citizens Advice Bureau

◆ Consumer Advice Centres

◆ Consumers' Association

◆ Local Authority Departments

Legislation to protect the consumer:

◆ Sale and Supply of Goods to Consumers Regulations 2002

◆ Consumer Protection for Unfair Trading Regulations 2008

◆ Food Safety Act 1990

◆ The Food Hygiene (Scotland) Regulations 2006

Chapter 8

MANAGEMENT OF EXPENDITURE

It can be difficult to 'make ends meet'. You get your weekly or monthly wage and before you realise it, it is gone. If this is how you feel, then it is probably time that you created a household budget. The principle of a good budget is that you either:

◆ balance your income and expenditure, or

◆ balance your income and expenditure by putting your spare income into a savings account.

The starting point is to make a list of your income. This income can be fixed (does not change on a regular basis) or variable (changes on a frequent basis). Table 8.1 lists what can be considered income.

Income	Fixed	Variable	Notes
Salary	x		If you are paid per hour worked and your hours vary, then this may be variable.
Partner's salary	x		If your partner is paid per hour worked and their hours vary, then this may be variable.
Guaranteed overtime	x		Can be fixed or variable depending on hours worked. Do not include overtime if this is not regular.
Pensions	x		This is an amount of money paid out if you have retired. Tends to be fixed.
Child Benefit	x		This is an amount of money paid to you by the government if you have children still in education or training. This is a fixed amount.
Income Support	x		This is an amount of money paid to you by the government if you have a low income. This is a fixed amount.
Tax Credit	x		This is an amount of money paid to you by the government if you have a low income. This is a fixed amount.
Other benefits	x		This is an amount of money paid to you by the government for a variety of different situations. This is a fixed amount.
Interest		x	Amount paid out by a bank for saving money.
Maintenance	x		This is an amount of money paid to you by a partner if you no longer live together. This is a usually a fixed amount.

Table 8.1 Common types of income

It is best to create budgets only on income that is fixed.

The next part is to identify your outgoings, or expenditure. Expenditure can be fixed or variable just like income, but can also be essential (E), which absolutely needs to be paid, or non essential (NE), meaning you could probably do without this expenditure if you needed to cut back.

	F	V	E	NE	Notes
Mortgage/Rent	x		x		
Council tax	x		x		
House insurance	x		x		
Fuel- electricity/gas/oil/coal		x	x		Can be regarded as fixed if you pay a fixed monthly amount.
Telephone		x		x	Now regarded as essential.
TV licence	x		x		Essential if you have a TV.
Car MOT	x		x		Essential if you have a car.
Road tax	x		x		Essential if you have a car.
Personal insurance	x			x	Not classified as essential.
Maintenance payments	x		x		Essential if required to pay as this is a legal obligation.
Loan/HP/credit repayments	x		x		Essential as these are legal documents.
School fees	x			x	
Food		x	x		
Pocket money	x			x	
Childminder	x		x		May be essential due to work commitments.
Toys and books		x		x	
Pet food		x	x	x	Essential if you own a pet.
Alcohol		x		x	
Public transport		x	x	x	Essential if you need to travel to work.
Cigarettes	x			x	
Magazines and newspapers	x			x	
Holidays		x		x	
House repairs		x	x		Essential to ensure a safe and protected home.
Clothing		x		x	
Meals out		x		x	
Furniture		x		x	

Table 8.2 Common types of expenditures

If the difference between your income and expenditure is positive, this means that you have extra money that you can save. But if the difference between your income and expenditure is negative, then this means you may be falling into debt.

It is good to look at the pattern of your spending over time. If there is a negative pattern overall, you will need to consider **maximising your income** and **making changes to your spending habits** – in other words, reducing your expenditure.

Maximising your income can be achieved in different ways:

◆ Increasing your earning, such as by working extra hours or taking a second job. This may not be easy to do.

◆ Reducing the amount of tax you pay by claiming appropriate tax credits. You may be entitled to tax credits that you don't know about, or none at all. (The CAB would be able to advise you on this.)

◆ Claiming for the benefits to which you are entitled. As with taxes, you may or may not be entitled to any additional benefits. (The CAB would be able to advise you on this.)

It can be difficult to increase your income. It is easier to try to reduce those areas of expenditure which are **not essential**, such as magazines, newspapers, alcohol and holidays. You can also try to reduce your spending on essential items by following some of the suggestions below:

Food:

◆ Take a packed lunch to school or work rather than paying higher prices for shop or canteen meals.

◆ Make a shopping list and stick to it – this prevents buying unnecessary items.

◆ Use money off coupons from papers, magazines and loyalty schemes when possible.

Insurance, fuel, telephone:

◆ Go to web comparison sites like www.moneysupermarket.com to find the cheapest supplier of these services and switch suppliers if necessary.

Transport:

◆ Try to use one car or even car share, if possible, to reduce fuel bills.

◆ Use public transport, walk or cycle as an alternative.

◆ Undertake vehicle maintenance yourself, if possible, to reduce maintenance costs.

Entertainment/recreation:

◆ Try to participate in activities that are free and nearby – this will reduce expenditure on this budget item and you will not have to pay any travel costs.

HOW TO PASS STANDARD GRADE HOME ECONOMICS

Housing:

◆ Undertake DIY for those repairs that you would be able to do yourself.

◆ Shop carefully for appliances and furniture, making use of sales when possible.

Example

The monthly expenditure of the Smith family is shown in the chart below.

The family needs to make changes to their expenditure due to a drop in their household income.

Choose **two** non-essential areas of expenditure and **one** essential area of expenditure and, for each, explain how expenditure could be reduced.

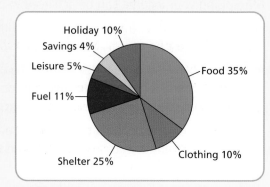

Figure 8.1

This is a 6 mark KU Credit question. You are allocated a mark for identifying correct areas of expenditure and a further mark for each explanation as to how expenditure might be reduced. Although this is a KU question, your selection of essential and non-essential areas of expenditure must come from the chart provided.

Sample answers:

Non-essential areas of expenditure

Holidays

◆ *Holidays are a luxury and as such the spending from this area could be severely reduced/stopped until the situation was rectified.*

◆ *A cheaper holiday could be planned that would mean less money was required and so some funds could be diverted to essential areas of expenditure.*

Savings

◆ *The money already saved under this category could be diverted to solving some of the problems encountered by the drop in income.*

◆ *Money could be transferred to a higher interest/locked savings account to protect what was there until additional savings could be guaranteed.*

Example *continued* ➢

> **Example** *continued*

C | *Leisure*

- *The family could take part in leisure activities that were cheaper e.g. go to local authority leisure facilities rather than private facilities.*
- *All non-essential spending e.g. subscriptions should be temporarily suspended/stopped/cancelled to ensure savings were made.*

Fuel

(you may interpret this as fuel linked to transport/car and as such could be classed as non-essential)

- *The family can limit/reduce spending in this area greatly by choosing alternative forms of transport, such as the bus, which may be cheaper.*
- *The family can opt for free forms of transport like walking/cycling as long as the distances involved are not prohibitive.*

Essential area of expenditure

Food

- *The family could buy foods from discount stores to ensure food costs are reduced.*
- *Cook food at home rather than go for take away meals/eat out as this tends to be a cheaper option.*

Clothing

- *The family could buy from charity shops/second-hand shops to reduce overall expenditure.*
- *The family could pass clothing from one child to another to save on clothing expenditure.*

Shelter

- *If having to maintain the property/undertake repairs, the family could shop around for the best price/deal/service.*
- *Depending on their mortgage deal, the family may be able to suspend a payment or try for a different or lower rate mortgage.*

Fuel

- *The family could stop draughts and heat escaping through floorboards and skirting boards by filling gaps with newspaper, beading or sealant.*
- *The family could turn their thermostat down by 1°C, as it could cut their heating bills by up to 10%.*

Example

C A much shorter budgeting question might look like the Credit KU question below. This relies on your ability to recall information.

Explain each of the following budgeting terms:

Balanced budget

Fixed income.

Sample answers:

♦ *A balanced budget is one where the total income of the household equals the total expenditure of the household.*

♦ *Fixed income is the amount of income that comes into a home which does not fluctuate in value/remains constant over time.*

1 mark would be allocated to the explanation of each term to total 2 marks.

Purchasing Goods and Services

When buying goods and services you can pay by cash or by credit. Credit is where you purchase goods and services on the basis that you will make payment in the future. This is normally regulated by some form of contract.

Method of payment	Advantages	Disadvantages
Cash	♦ You can only buy what you can afford. ♦ Easy and convenient way to pay for goods and services.	♦ Cash can be lost. ♦ Cash can be stolen. ♦ Cannot purchase items if you have not got sufficient cash.
Credit	♦ Can buy goods and services even when you do not have sufficient cash. ♦ Easy and convenient way to pay for goods and services. ♦ Prevents having to carry cash. ♦ Some forms of credit can offer you additional protection, e.g. credit cards, should purchased goods or service become faulty. ♦ Useful for emergencies like unexpected car repair.	♦ Card can be stolen and used fraudulently. ♦ You may have to pay interest if you do not pay off your credit at the end of each month. ♦ You may not be eligible for credit if you are under 18 or on a low income. ♦ It is easy to spend more than you can afford to pay back.

Table 8.3

Example

F The following Foundation KU question relates to the advantages and disadvantages of buying goods on cash and credit. It relies on your ability to recall information; 1 mark is awarded for an advantage and 1 mark for a disadvantage. In this question, the fact that the person is buying a jacket is not really important.

A student is planning to buy a new jacket.

List **one** advantage and **one** disadvantage of paying for the jacket by cash.

Sample answers:

Advantages

◆ *You can only buy a jacket according to the funds that you have available so you will not get into debt.*

◆ *It is an easy/convenient method of payment for the jacket.*

◆ *All shops will accept cash and so you should have no problems trying to buy a jacket.*

Disadvantages

◆ *Carrying large amounts of cash about is not always safe.*

◆ *Can be easy to lose money if not careful.*

◆ *You may be limited to the range of jackets available as you can only buy up to the total amount of money you have available.*

Key Words *and* Definitions

EFTPOS – Electronic Fund Transfer at Point Of Sale: term for using a card to pay for goods and services.

When paying by cash, you can pay using a variety of different methods, each with positive and negative aspects:

Debit card

- cash is placed into a bank account
- bank issues a cash card
- cash card used to pay for goods and services at the point of sale
- card can be used to withdraw money from ATMs
- can only spend the amount of money that you have in your bank account.

Direct debit

- cash is paid into bank account
- form completed to allow regular payment for goods or services that are usually weekly/monthly/quarterly/yearly and for a fixed or variable amount, such as Council tax or gym memberships
- payment made direct to the company by the bank from your bank account
- payment will not be made if you do not have sufficient money in your account (with possible fee charged)
- if direct debit has been incorrectly paid the bank has to refund your money.

Key Words *and* Definitions

Standing Order: your bank sends a fixed amount of money to the beneficiary.

Direct Debit: the beneficiary claims the money from your bank account.

Standing order – similar to a direct debit, but for a fixed amount.

When paying by credit you can pay using a variety of different methods. As with cash, there are positive and negative aspects to using credit cards:

Credit card

- bank or finance company issues a credit card
- credit card used to pay for goods and services at the point of sale
- card can be used to withdraw money from ATMs
- you have to apply for a credit card and meet certain criteria e.g. over 18 years old, have a good credit history and a sufficient income to cover repayments
- you may have to pay a yearly charge for your credit card, other offer these free
- you are provided with an account balance monthly
- usually you have to pay a minimum of £5 or 5% of the balance
- you pay interest on any balance not paid which can vary from 0% to as high as 35% APR

HOW TO PASS STANDARD GRADE HOME ECONOMICS

◆ you are provided with some protection should a business from which you have bought faulty goods stop trading; purchases must be between £100 and £30,000 in value

◆ protection also applies to buying faulty goods where the retailer refuses to provide a refund

◆ some cards offer an initial 0% interest rate for a fixed period of time

◆ you can swap card providers and pay off the balance of one credit card using the other credit card, although this is not good practice

◆ can be used around the world.

Key Words *and* Definitions

APR – Annual Percentage Rate: figure that gives you the total cost of credit including interest and other administrative charges. The lower the APR, the lower the charges.

Charge card – As with a credit card, but you have to pay the full balance at the end of the month.

Store cards

These are the same as for credit cards, but you can use these cards only in the stores that belong to the company offering the card like Marks and Spencer or JJB. Store cards may have a high APR.

There are two types of store account:

◆ monthly account – operates in the same way as a credit card in that you are charged interest if you do not pay your monthly balance in full

◆ budget account – you agree to pay back a monthly amount and this determines your credit limit.

Credit sale

◆ buy goods at the cash price

◆ you pay interest at a set fee

◆ you may be able to get interest free credit

◆ repayment is made in regular instalments

◆ you own the goods as soon as you sign the contract

◆ the supplier of the goods cannot take the goods away from you if you do not make your payments. They can, however, take you to court

◆ there is a 'cooling off' period with any credit sale – usually 7 days, if you signed the agreement anywhere other than the premises of the supplier or if you discussed the credit face to face with the supplier before signing the agreement.

Hire Purchase

Similar to a credit sale, but with important differences:

◆ You are hiring the goods and you do not own the goods until you make the final payment.

◆ You can end the agreement and return the goods at any time, although there may be some financial penalties if you do this.

◆ The company providing the HP can repossess the goods if you fall behind with repayments.

◆ The company will require a court order to repossess goods.

Questions *and* Answers

Mary is **starting university** and wants to **open a bank account**. Mary wants to be able to **manage her money easily** and she plans **not to get into debt**. Mary will be **travelling abroad** for a year as part of her course.

Study the information about bank accounts below.

Choose **one** bank account and **evaluate** its suitability for Mary.

Bank account A	Bank account B
◆ Free banking – provided you stay in credit or within your agreed overdraft limit ◆ Free automatic overdraft facility of £100 ◆ Apply for up to £1,250 interest-free overdraft facility in your first year ◆ 1.5% interest paid on money in your account ◆ A debit card and cheque guarantee card allowing 24 hour access to cash machines* ◆ Free 24 hour telephone banking that lets you check your balance, review recent transactions, pay regular bills, order cheque books ◆ Free financial advice ◆ Branches located at or near most major universities *subject to available funds in the account	◆ Interest free overdraft of up to £2,000 depending on which year of study you are in ◆ A free credit card with a credit limit of up to £500 and up to 8 weeks interest free credit ◆ 1.9% interest paid on money in your account ◆ Debit card allowing 24 hour access to cash machines ◆ Register for Digi Banking* ◆ 20% off selected books, and discounts off CDs, DVDs, tapes, videos and computer games ◆ Debit card allows you to use cash machines and pay for goods and services abroad ◆ Free financial advice *Internet banking service lets you use your computer to do all your banking needs

Questions and *Answers continued* ➢

MANAGEMENT OF EXPENDITURE

Questions and Answers continued

This Credit level HI question uses banking as the context for the information to be evaluated. With this question, you get no marks for the selection of the bank account, because this is an evaluation question; you get marks for explaining why the bank account is, or is not, suitable for Mary.

Sample answers:

Bank account A

- ◆ *Free banking is good for Mary as she will be starting university and money might be tight so this will save her money.*

- ◆ *Free overdraft of £1,250 might be useful to Mary should she find that being a student is financially difficult and she needs additional funds in year 1.*

- ◆ *The 1.5% interest may not be as good as other banks and so Mary might be losing some cash, which might be important if she is struggling financially.*

- ◆ *The debit card allows 24 hour access to her money and Mary wants to be able to manage her money easily so can get bank statements/balances when she wants.*

- ◆ *The cheque guarantee card means that Mary can use cheques as a means of payment when she has no cash on her so making life easier for her.*

- ◆ *There are branches near most universities and so the bank should be near enough to Mary to allow her to manage her money easily.*

Bank account B

- ◆ *The up to £2,000 free overdraft might be useful to Mary should she find that being a student is financially difficult and she needs additional funds in any given year.*

- ◆ *The free credit card might be of value to Mary as she will be able to use it to buy purchases without going into debt if she uses it wisely/within the 8 week interest free credit period.*

- ◆ *Mary will accumulate additional money due to the interest paid on her bank balance and so will aid her desire not to get into debt.*

- ◆ *Mary can register for Digi Banking which will allow her to keep track of her finances easily.*

- ◆ *The discount off selected books etc. may be of use to Mary if she has to buy student materials for her course and this will save her money so perhaps preventing debt.*

- ◆ *The debit card can be used abroad which is ideal for Mary as this means she can access money/accounts when she is travelling abroad.*

Questions and Answers continued ➤

HOW TO PASS STANDARD GRADE HOME ECONOMICS

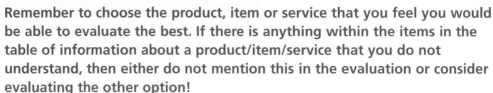

Questions and **Answers** continued

Remember to choose the product, item or service that you feel you would be able to evaluate the best. If there is anything within the items in the table of information about a product/item/service that you do not understand, then either do not mention this in the evaluation or consider evaluating the other option!

Problems with credit

It may be that you try to obtain credit but are refused. **Credit Reference Agencies** are organisations that keep a record of your credit transactions so that companies that wish to offer credit can check to see how much of a 'risk' you might be. If you have problems with making your monthly payments on utility items or credit cards, you may have a poor credit rating.

With all the credit that is available, it is not surprising that people get into debt. Table 8.5 provides advice on how to manage debt and prevent more from building.

Step	Action required
1	Do not take out any other forms of credit.
2	Make a list of all your debts.
3	Work out your budget so see what you can afford to pay your creditors.
4	Deal with priority debts first e.g. mortgage/rent, fuel, council tax, court fines, tax arrears, loans, HP.
5	Deal then with non-priority debts e.g. overdrafts, personal loans, credit cards.
6	Do not ignore letters from creditors – the problem will not go away.
7	Contact creditors to make them aware of your situation – they may be able to offer reduced monthly payments or even freeze your interest for a period of time.
8	Offer reduced payments based on your budget from step 3 above.
9	It is advisable to seek assistance from experts such as: ◆ Citizens advice Bureau – see page 132 ◆ Trading Standards Department – see page 133 ◆ Consumer Credit Counselling Service – a charity that offers free advice and assistance.

Table 8.5

Example

G This 3 mark KU question uses debt prevention as the theme but links to budgeting. A mark is awarded for each step detailed for one of the areas given.

A family have been advised by a debt advisor to reduce spending in each of the following areas:

transport

entertainment for the children.

Detail **three** steps that the family could take to reduce expenditure in **one** of the areas.

Sample answers:

Transport

◆ *Use public transport instead of a car as public transport tends to be cheaper.*

◆ *Use a bicycle/moped/scooter/motor bike rather than a car to get to work as this may be cheaper to maintain/run than a car.*

◆ *Car share/organise school run/trips with friends/neighbours/work mates in order to limit the amount of time that the car has to be used.*

Entertainment for the children

◆ *Rather than use commercial entertainment use free entertainment when available in order to reduce expenditure e.g. public museums.*

◆ *Organise entertainment in the home/garden/park in order to reduce outlay of fee paying activities.*

◆ *Unsubscribe from subscription services for TV which can cause added expenditure.*

In this type of question where you have a choice within the question, think carefully about which option to choose. Choose the area that you know most about.

Summary

What you need to know!

Sources of household income

Sources of household expenditure

Principles of budgeting

Priorities when budgeting

Methods of payment:

◆ Cash and cash payment types

◆ Credit and credit payment types

Credit reference agencies

Debt management